THE CONFIDENCE EQUATION

Three Keys to Unleashing Self-Confidence as an Introvert

DAN ROSENFELD

Health Communications, Inc.
Mt. Pleasant, South Carolina

www.hcibooks.com

Library of Congress Cataloging-in-Publication Data
is available through the Library of Congress

ISBN-13: 978-07573-2606-6 (Paperback)
ISBN-10: 07573-2606-4 (Paperback)
ISBN-13: 978-07573-2607-3 (ePub)
ISBN-10: 07573-2607-2 (ePub)

Publisher: Health Communications, Inc.
1240 Winnowing Way, Suite 102
Mt. Pleasant, SC 29466

Cover design by Josh Rosenfeld
Interior design, and formatting by Larissa Hise Henoch

CONTENTS

INTRODUCTION

As I drove across Los Angeles, I knew I'd be several hours early for my 7:00 PM showtime. That night was the final round of the U.S. Comedy Contest, and I was one of six comedians left competing for the first-place national title.

I'd started dabbling in stand-up comedy only a few months earlier and was frankly shocked that the judges had voted me through. I didn't enter this contest looking to win; I just wanted to challenge myself to do something out of my comfort zone. And out of my comfort zone I sure was—an introvert with almost no performing experience, attempting to make a room of two hundred strangers laugh.

I wasn't a natural showman. I wasn't a performer type. And, in my eyes, I wasn't even a real comedian. I was just a guy happy to get experience telling jokes somewhere other than his living room.

On my way to the venue, I rehearsed my five-minute set over and over again. I'd meticulously crafted and memorized 584 words: vocal inflections, pauses, accompanying gestures, and all. I gave my set a beautiful story arc with an exposition, climax, and resolution. Each word cued the next in my mind, timed perfectly to end at four minutes and fifty-nine seconds with effortless recitation. A hair within the contest's five-minute limit, each word in my set chosen with intentionality and purpose.

I arrived by 5:00 PM, my mind dancing between calm and excitement. I felt confident knowing my set was ingrained in my memory. Memorizing my script word for word was my cheat code: It meant I could recite it onstage without thinking, allowing me to dissociate from reality and ease my anxiety. I had a five-minute mental script I could mindlessly regurgitate, and that was all I needed. Easy.

Until it wasn't.

At 6:30 that evening, the contest director called all the comedians together, reviewed the night's lineup, and announced, "As you all know, you'll each have three minutes for your set, and we'll be strictly enforcing this time limit. So, when you see the light flash by the back wall, that's your thirty-second warning to wrap up. Good luck!"

Panic ensued. Well, one person was panicking. Me.

While my fellow comedians seemed well aware of the three-minute protocol, I'd spent the past four months living in a delusional world carefully memorizing a set word for word of not three, not four, but five minutes. Apparently, all for naught, as my set—the *only* set I'd ever written—was no longer usable.

I considered my options, and they all sucked. Cutting the last two minutes of my set would ruin the whole story arc, like watching a movie that ends abruptly. Exposition, some climax, but no resolution. Not happening.

I also knew I couldn't shorten my set by just cutting out two minutes of material elsewhere. I had memorized my set in such a way that each word cued the next in my mind. Remove any part of the set, and those vital cues were gone. My performance would fall apart as I'd stand onstage fumbling for words.

I felt defeated, with no way out. I'd spent months building up my confidence for this night by preparing as much as I could: writing, memorizing, and rehearsing, over and over again. I drilled my set into my mind like holy scripture. This meticulous preparation was my lifeline, a way to step out of my introverted self and become the fearless performer I felt I wasn't. Now, a half hour before showtime, I had no performance to deliver at all.

Just when I was ready to throw in the towel, forfeit my spot in the contest, and drive home, a thought struck me: So what if I bombed onstage? Wasn't the whole point of entering this contest to challenge myself? Sure, the stakes felt high—there were ten celebrity judges in the room, two hundred strangers staring at the stage, and who knows how many viewers tuning in to the live stream from home. But I wasn't doing this for any of them. I was doing it for myself.

At that moment, I saw this was an opportunity to challenge the restrictions I'd placed on myself as a comedian. I'd always relied on memorizing a script to be confident onstage, but tonight, I wanted my confidence to come not from my memory but from being comfortable with who I am as a person. My entire set was about the struggles I'd faced growing up with a disability and how I could always find hope and humor no matter the adversity. How was this night any different?

I threw away my set notes, walked onto the stage, and spoke from the heart. I opened with a joke about the irony of myself performing *stand-up* comedy when, as a kid, I was so disabled I could barely *stand up.* The joke bombed spectacularly, met with blank stares and uncomfortable squirms. To this day, I can't remember anything I said after that, except for my next line: "You guys know it's okay to laugh, right?"

Two hours later, I drove home with a first-place trophy riding shotgun in my car.

HOW IT ALL BEGAN . . .

I didn't always have a confident side. In fact, the early years of my life were anything but.

On June 20, 1996, I was rushed from my mother's embrace into the ICU. Beat by beat, my heart fought to see the end of a long summer day in New York—the second longest day of any year, in fact, and the longest day of my life.

My birth was a rough one, setting the stage for the struggles I'd face growing up.

When I was born, I almost died. During my delivery, oxygen stopped flowing to my brain for some time. As it turns out, that small window of time was enough to cause a few weeks of agony in the ICU and a lifetime of damage ahead. In those few moments, I suffered a brain injury that permanently damaged my cerebral motor cortex. That cortex is a big player in the brain—because it's the part that allows you to move your muscles around.

Within my first few seconds of life, I lost access to a future where I could control how my body functions. I exchanged years of freedom for years of physical rehabilitation. I lost hope for a life where I would ever feel comfortable in my own skin. I developed a lifelong physical disability called cerebral palsy.

I spent my first few weeks on an ICU bed, fighting to survive each day. It's a miracle I left the hospital alive.

Cerebral palsy in a human body is like a mechanical malfunction in a new car. You know all the parts *should* be working fine and you *should* feel the car accelerate when you step on the gas. But something feels . . . clunky. The car accelerates in random bursts. It makes strange noises. And it doesn't go nearly as fast as you know it should. It's as if the engine is missing a part, and the harder you step on the gas, the more you feel the car resist your foot's instructions.

My body doesn't like to accelerate. Not metaphorically and certainly not physically.

I've faced and overcome all kinds of challenges throughout my life. Growing up, I spent dozens of hours in physical therapy learning how to walk. I spent hundreds of hours in speech therapy learning how to talk. And I spent thousands of hours in occupational therapy learning how to do tasks that usually don't need much formal learning—like tying my own shoes, buckling a seatbelt, and holding a pencil the right way.

Cerebral palsy wasn't something I dealt with only in physical or occupational therapy. It was with me all day, every day. Everywhere I went, my disability followed. For most of my childhood, I walked around with corrective braces on my legs. Leg braces were my normal, and I knew that I couldn't walk very well without them. Hand splints were part of my nightly pajamas, as each night before bed I'd bandage my hands and arms as though they'd just been broken. Until I was ten years old, my parents pushed me around in a stroller almost everywhere we went during family outings. If our plans involved walking around for more than a few minutes, I was bound to a stroller. Walking more than a quarter mile just wasn't an option.

I didn't even notice the strangeness of it all until I was in elementary school. I felt like the other kids I knew at school lived in bodies that had been inspected and tuned. My body, meanwhile, was missing parts and came with a DIY—do it yourself—manual.

As it turns out, I'm a DIY kind of guy.

By writing my own DIY manual and living life with my own flair, I've overcome barriers and developed a deep sense of confidence. I came into this world with two uncooperative hands, two unstable legs, and several hundred spastic muscles from head to toe. Each day, I've walked around with an awkward pep and uncoordinated limbs that have garnered stares, raised eyebrows, and prompted plenty of questions. Yet, throughout my life, I've nurtured a love for who I am and a belief in what I could become.

In my life, I've become a psychologist, scientist, entrepreneur, dating coach, university lecturer, author, comedian, actor, and professional athlete. I've earned a PhD, founded my own company, won a national stand-up comedy contest, traveled the world as a member of the U.S. National Paralympic Table Tennis Team, and won a gold medal at the U.S. Open Table Tennis Championships. (Yes, there's a U.S. Open for table tennis.) And despite all that, I still struggle to tie my shoes each day and can't even write my own name legibly.

As an introvert, I've looked inward to navigate life's challenges and develop my own brand of confidence. Confidence is often seen through the lens of extroverted traits, like being outgoing, sociable, and assertive. But for introverts, confidence manifests differently. It involves deep self-reflection, self-acceptance, and self-regulation. It means overcoming self-doubt and reprogramming your inner dialogue to build you up, not break you down. It requires a strategic approach to vulnerability, an adaptive form of resilience, and an inquisitive journey toward self-discovery. Introverts build confidence, not by striving to match outgoing, extroverted ideals, but by cultivating self-awareness and finding strength in their individuality.

Through the ups and downs of my journey with cerebral palsy, I've learned a lot about what it means to be confident. I've learned how to make the most of life when it feels as though all odds are stacked against me. And through getting a PhD in psychology, I've learned how to understand my experiences with true insight and to appreciate the deeper lessons they provide about human nature. This is my story and the life lessons I've gained—from ICU to PhD, and everything in between.

Science is based on experimentation, and my life has been one heck of an experiment so far. Along the way, I've tested what works, what fails, and what fuels real confidence. Out of that messy personal data, I've created something simple: an equation. A formula you can use to unleash self confidence.

Follow along. You deserve it.

THE CONFIDENCE EQUATION

Developing confidence is a personal journey of learning how to express yourself and pursue your goals without self-doubt. It requires a true desire to step into confidence and an acceptance that you are deserving. Ultimately, for introverts, it comes from applying the following equation:

Strategic Vulnerability
+ Adaptive Resilience
+ Inquisitive Self-Discovery

CONFIDENCE

These three keys—vulnerability, resilience, and self-discovery—unlock your inner confidence. When you embrace your vulnerabilities strategically, adapt to challenges through resilience, and rediscover yourself inquisitively, you quiet your self-doubt and unleash a deep belief in who you are.

Confidence isn't something you stumble upon by coincidence. You don't just wake up with it out of the blue. It's a trait you can deliberately nurture by targeting the three keys that make up the confidence equation.

GIVING YOURSELF THE GIFT OF CONFIDENCE

I see confidence as a gift—and what a beautiful gift it is. Being confident brings all kinds of benefits. Confident people are happier. They're better at overcoming challenges and feel less stressed or anxious than others. They're more ambitious in their hobbies, more successful in their careers, and more comfortable navigating tough decisions about work and life. They enjoy stronger relationships, better sex, and deeper friendships. They really have it all.

The thing about confidence, though, is that it's not a gift anyone else can grant to you. It's a gift only you can give yourself.

In this book, you'll learn how to gift yourself the confidence you deserve. You'll learn that your own brand of authentic confidence already exists within you, and that it's just a matter of knowing how to bring it to the surface. Most of all, you'll learn that confidence isn't something you need to work hard to achieve. You don't need to buy a new wardrobe, start a new exercise plan, chant any daily affirmations, climb Mount Everest, pretend to be extroverted, or change anything about yourself and who you are right now. You just need to think about your life a bit differently, and I'll show you exactly how, each step of the way.

This book is about how I found confidence through strategic vulnerability, adaptive resilience, and inquisitive self-discovery—and how you can too. The twelve chapters ahead cover twelve life lessons about confidence, tailored specifically for introverts. They're organized into three sections: one for each key of the confidence equation. We'll start by taking a deep dive into strategic vulnerability and the power of opening up to the world around you. Then we'll tackle the two other keys to confidence: adaptive resilience and inquisitive self-discovery.

Along the way, I'll invite you to reflect deeply, think critically, and challenge old stories you've told yourself. To get the most out of this process, I recommend keeping a dedicated journal as you read. Jot down your reactions and reflections as they arise. Writing things down is powerful; it turns insight into action and nurtures the seeds of personal growth. After all, confidence isn't just something you read about. It's something you build, one insight at a time.

In each chapter, you'll hear personal stories from my experiences with table tennis, stand-up comedy, and cerebral palsy, along with a psychological analysis of what these stories reveal and the lessons they offer. Think of this book as my personal diary turned into a PhD dissertation of psychoanalysis—all for your benefit.

You're welcome.

KEY #1
STRATEGIC VULNERABILITY

Chapter 1

YOUR DIFFERENCES ARE ASSETS

When I was in elementary school, I remember some of my classmates getting braces to straighten out their teeth. They felt self-conscious about their mouthful of metal, worried about what other kids would think and say about them. I found their fears all too familiar.

While my classmates worried about how they'd look with braces on their teeth, I spent my childhood with corrective braces on my legs. While my classmates worried about solving the problems on our math tests, I worried whether I could even hold my pencil the right way. And while my classmates hoped they were wearing the "cool" pair of shoes that year, I was in occupational therapy hoping this would be the year I could finally tie my own shoes.

Throughout my life, I've felt different—like I don't fit in. As I've aged, however, I've learned that my differences aren't weaknesses;

they're perspectives. They shape how I view the world around me, navigating that world with a distinct sense of identity. They're the qualities that make me unique, resilient, empathetic, lighthearted, self-assured, and self-aware. Why fight against my differences in hopes of suppressing them when I can instead appreciate them as strengths and unlock their real value?

A mental shift like this can be incredibly empowering, especially for introverts. Introverts often feel different because they prefer periods of alone time over constant togetherness or smaller gatherings over huge parties. These social preferences are readily misunderstood and stigmatized in cultures that glorify extroversion as an ideal. When constant chatter feels like the norm, retreating inward to be with yourself gets labeled as "weird." When going out feels like the standard for social success, wanting to stay in can feel like a social deficiency. However, embracing these preferences as strengths, rather than weaknesses, can transform how you feel about your self-worth and how you navigate social expectations.

Embracing my differences through this mental shift has allowed me to excel in every aspect of my life, introversion and well beyond. Rather than fighting my oddities, I've accepted and owned the full spectrum of who I am as a person with cerebral palsy, quirks and all. My ability to play any sport with my own adaptive flair is a testament to my creativity, and the awkward way I walk is a reminder of my ability to feel comfortable in myself no matter how others view me.

I've stopped trying to fit into molds that were never meant for me.

I've stopped trying to fit into molds that were never meant for me. Instead, I've embraced my unique way of living and the perspective it's given me. This mentality has underpinned my success in school, work, and especially table tennis.

I've been competing in table tennis at a high level for over a decade. As a two-time U.S. Open gold medalist, former U.S. National Team member, and nationally certified coach, I've poured thousands of hours into honing my craft, learning from some of the best players and coaches in the world. Yet, despite all this dedication, there's one thing I still can't do: hit a proper backhand.

My forehand? It's polished, powerful, and picture-perfect. But my backhand? You know, the other foundational skill of my sport? Downright abysmal—at least by conventional standards.

In table tennis, the forehand and backhand use totally different muscles in your body, and while I have decently developed forehand muscles, my cerebral palsy weakens my backhand muscles much more. To this day, I can't hit a proper backhand the way you're "supposed to." It feels awkward, weak, and uncoordinated. I just don't have the shoulder mobility or strength to pull it off, and I likely never will.

For years, this deficit frustrated me. I compensated for it by developing a strange way of hitting my backhand that used other muscles in my body. I could get the ball over the net, but my form was idiosyncratic and looked nothing like it should. My form was *weird*. So, I spent hundreds more hours working to correct my technique with top coaches, but while my forehand kept getting better and better, my "proper" backhand stayed the same. Weak and ineffective. This persistent struggle eventually led me to a crucial realization: My strange backhand, in all of its strangeness, wasn't a curse; it might just be my greatest asset.

It took some time but in my early twenties, I finally made a radical shift in my mindset. Rather than trying to get rid of the parts of my table tennis game that seemed different, I started to embrace my idiosyncrasies and turn them into strengths. I stopped working to correct my backhand technique and instead worked on making its strangeness even stranger.

The stranger I let my backhand become, the more it started catching my opponents off guard, as they hadn't seen anything like it before. While it wasn't the "best" backhand they'd faced, it was surely the most surprising. That element of surprise became my secret weapon.

THE PRESSURE TO CONFORM

By embracing my physical difference, I transformed it from a hindrance into an asset of my table tennis game. Outside of table tennis, my physical differences have been uncomfortable. Growing up, I was self-conscious about my body—the way I walked, how deformed my hands looked, and the way my legs looked wrapped up in braces.

Like many of us, I learned to strive for conformity from an early age. Fitting in felt safe while being different felt marginalized. I remember the faces of countless strangers who've stared at me in public, wondering why I look different. As a ten-year-old being pushed around in a stroller by my parents, I felt their eyes upon me signaling my status as different.

All around us, there's a social pressure to conform. This pressure is part of being human. Introverts often feel this pressure keenly as society tends to prize extroverted qualities like seemingly effortless sociability and assertiveness. When you deviate from the norm—whether in your personality, appearance, ability, or beliefs—people tend to view you as an outsider or as less capable, often questioning your worth. Our minds are so attuned to social feedback that we pick up on these cues acutely, no matter how subtle they seem. Sadly, this can erode our ability to feel confident.

For many people, this begins early in life. Children who appear or act differently from their peers may be teased or socially excluded, planting the seeds of self-doubt in their minds. These early life experiences can crystallize into a deep-seated belief that their differences make them inferior, instilling in them a mindset of self-doubt as they grow older. It shouldn't be this way—and it doesn't have to be.

CELEBRATING YOUR DIFFERENCES

From a young age, introverts face pressures to conform to extroverted norms. We're taught to feel self-conscious about preferring solitude or smaller, shorter gatherings. While these preferences on their own are normal, healthy, and common, they face scrutiny in cultures that prize extroversion. The world's judgment seeps in, becoming a quiet voice in your head that whispers, "I'm not enough." As a result, introverts are left feeling marginalized for being themselves. We feel like there's something wrong with us, simply because we're different.

Worrying about your differences and seeking to fit in is one of the most powerful threats to confidence. It prevents you from meeting your basic need for self-acceptance, which is fundamental to psychological well-being. It holds you back from recognizing, embracing, and valuing all aspects of yourself without judgment, including your strengths *and* your weaknesses. It stops you from feeling that you're inherently worthy and valuable as an individual. Most of all, it trains your mind to view other people's rejections of who you are as your own rejections of yourself.

When you become conditioned to suppress your differences in hopes of fitting in, you deny your authenticity and start to question yourself. This suppression can lead to internal conflict as the person you present to the world becomes increasingly disconnected from your true self. Life becomes more and more a performance, and the more you perform, the less you express your truth—to others or to yourself.

Almost everyone does this to some degree. But that doesn't make it any less harmful. Self-suppression creates a sense of inner turmoil and dissatisfaction that takes a heavy toll. We put up walls in our minds and lives to defend the most vulnerable parts of our identity from social rejection. We conceal many parts of who we are because our self-worth feels at risk when these parts of us surface into public view. We act how we see other people acting because, in the moment, it feels good to fit in. However, this temporary comfort comes at the cost of long-term fulfillment and self-acceptance. It brings feelings of isolation and loneliness as we feel that our true selves are neither seen nor appreciated. We deny ourselves the gift of self-expression.

The irony is that while suppressing your differences may *feel* like a surefire way to feel confident, it makes you feel just the opposite. It's a toxic way of thinking that flows from a pool of self-doubt. It makes you pretend to be someone you're not, stripping away your authenticity and your individuality.

Celebrating your differences, expressing yourself openly, and nurturing your individuality are crucial for feeling at ease in your own skin. When you embrace what sets you apart from others, you can show yourself the kind of care you naturally want from others. You can think more creatively and get more in touch with your unique qualities and strengths. You can make the most of your abilities. You can stop overthinking and start acting from your instincts.

For introverts, this means recognizing that trying to conform to extroverted ideals can be as counterproductive as trying to change any other part of yourself. It means embracing your introspective side, sensitivity, and comfort with solitude. This self-awareness and self-acceptance allow you to express yourself, pursue your goals, and tackle challenges with more belief in your abilities and more pride in who you are.

Introversion isn't a weakness; it's a different kind of strength.

YOUR ASSET ACTIVATION PLAN

Here are some steps you can take to start celebrating your differences, recognizing your assets, and activating them to their full potential.

1. **Reflect on Your Differences.** Spend time writing in a journal about what makes you unique. Make note of any qualities, preferences, experiences, perspectives, values, or goals that set you apart from others.
2. **Practice Gratitude.** Acknowledge that your differences might bring challenges, but don't stop there. Look beyond the struggles to discover the hidden strengths, insights, and opportunities they offer. After all, there are two sides to every coin. Make a list of these gifts that come from your differences, no matter how small or hidden they may be. Appreciate the ways in which your differences are assets. Replace feelings of insecurity with feelings of pride.
3. **Express Yourself Creatively.** Choose an outlet that resonates with you and lets you apply your differences in creative ways.

This could be painting, writing, dance, fashion, sports, or music—*anything* really. Find a way you can make it your own, pursuing it in a way unlike anyone else. For me, that creative self-expression shows up in two ways: playing table tennis with my quirky backhand and performing comedy, where I share personal stories about having a disability. The key theme? Stepping into your differences rather than fighting against them. Do things your way. Dedicate time each week to this activity and use it as a means to celebrate and express your individuality.

4. **Practice Self-Affirmation.** Each morning, look in the mirror and say three positive affirmations about your unique traits (for example, "I am thoughtful," "I am resilient," "I am brave") or something specific and purpose-driven like "I'm dedicated to sustainability." To deepen this practice, write down these affirmations in a journal and reflect on specific instances when these traits have benefited your life. This reinforces your belief in yourself and helps you internalize these affirmations more deeply.
5. **Seek Like-Minded Communities.** Join groups or forums where your differences are celebrated. This could be an online community, a club, a formal organization, or a support group where you can share your experiences and feel validated. It could even just be having a friend who champions your individuality.

As you celebrate your differences, you start to care less about what other people think and you listen more to your inner voice. You reinforce your sense of self-worth and foster a deeper confidence that comes from truly knowing, accepting, and loving who you are. As a result, you send a powerful message to yourself and others that you value and respect yourself, regardless of what social norms or external expectations tell you to think. This newfound authenticity allows you to stand tall and embrace your true self.

Celebrate your differences by changing how you view them. Instead of seeing them as flaws, redefine them as qualities that contribute to your individuality. Cherish the opportunities and achievements that have come from your unique traits. When you value your individuality, your differences aren't threats; they're what allow you to thrive.

EXPLOIT YOUR STRENGTHS

Born into poverty in rural Mississippi, Oprah Winfrey faced a mountain of challenges from a young age. Her rise to stardom, however, stemmed from her ability to exploit a strength she always had inside her: an ability to communicate and connect with people on a deeply emotional level.

Oprah's empathic demeanor and her gift for storytelling became her cornerstone, and she capitalized on them to the highest degree. Using her empathy and communication skills, she defined her own way of doing television.

Oprah's ability to exploit her strengths—her talent for making guests feel comfortable and understood—set her apart from her peers and redefined the talk show genre. Her differences became her greatest assets, propelling her from a local news anchor to one of the most influential media moguls in the world. She didn't just seek to fit in with the current media world; she transformed it by embracing her individuality and perspective.

Your individuality isn't just something to accept. It's something to exploit.

Exploiting your strengths can build confidence for any goals you pursue by reinforcing your individuality and reminding you of the power of your positive differences. Psychological research has shown that people who recognize and leverage their strengths tend to have higher levels of self-esteem and mental well-being. Your strengths are often tightly linked to your sense of identity, and exploiting your strengths makes you feel more secure in who you are. It reinforces your authentic self-worth.

In a world that often values social conformity, embracing your distinct strengths is a way to tell yourself that you value and respect the core qualities most central to who you are. This affirmation of your individuality helps you find direction and resilience in your self-worth. It makes you less inclined to seek validation or approval from other people. It makes your sense of confidence more internally anchored and robust.

Exploiting your strengths can also help you feel more confident by shifting your mind away from social comparison—the toxic habit that almost all of us can't help but do. The psychological study of social comparison theory explains how people determine their self-worth based on how they think they stack up against other people. This process of comparing yourself to others tends to make you feel inadequate, for the mind often has a self-defeating negativity bias. When you compare yourself to others, your mind makes you focus much more on your deficits and insecurities than on your talents and potential. It makes you feel less than.

However, when you intentionally focus on your own strengths, you shift your attention away from your social comparisons and toward a form of inner reflection. You stop thinking about ways in which you're inferior to others and instead you start appreciating what you bring to the table. The more unique your strengths are, the less you feel as though they're qualities you can even find in others, making them hard to compare socially at all. Cultivating your individuality in this way fosters a lasting belief in your worth that remains unthreatened by the successes of other people.

Your natural strengths give you a lot to work with. They're the talents and abilities you already have. Exploiting your strengths means taking those talents and abilities to the next level. It means viewing your natural strengths as a baseline level of ability with much more room to grow. It means working to realize their fullest potential.

When you exploit your strengths and develop the skills at which you're already talented, you open the door to psychological mastery. The more you succeed in applying and stretching your strengths, the more familiar you become with feelings of capability. That familiarity breeds a feeling of confidence. You arm yourself with talents that not only make you feel sufficient but let you truly excel.

BE THE OUTLIER

When you celebrate your differences, you start to see your individuality, not just as something to be accepted, but as positive qualities that set you apart. You take what others see as your flaws and turn them into your own assets. You can feel comfortable living life with your own flair. You can derive confidence from being an outlier.

Outliers don't just accept their uniqueness; they actively embrace it to pave new paths in the world. Being an outlier means challenging the status quo, thinking creatively, and approaching problems from fresh perspectives that others might overlook. It's a form of radical authenticity that empowers people to break free from conventional ways of doing things. When you embrace your differences, you're more likely to think outside the box and innovate.

Individuality is often a dormant gift waiting to be unwrapped. Consider Albert Einstein, for example, who was considered an outlier in both his personal life and the scientific community. As a child, Einstein faced challenges in school due to his unique way of thinking and learning. His teachers clashed with him because he didn't conform to their standard methods of learning and memorization. Instead, Einstein's mind was always questioning, probing more deeply. His style of thinking set him apart from his peers, and while he earned good grades, he was far from an exceptional student and often challenged the educational zeitgeist.

That same peculiar style of thinking eventually led Einstein toward groundbreaking scientific discoveries, which in themselves embodied an unapologetic uniqueness. Einstein's famed theory of relativity initially faced skepticism from other scientists. His ideas were so radical and different from the status quo that his peers found them difficult to accept. However, Einstein embraced his status as an outlier. He was comfortable stepping into this vulnerability and remained confident in himself and in his theories, furthering his unconventional way of seeing the world. His resilience and belief in his unique perspective ultimately paid off, and his theories went on to become cornerstones of modern physics.

In his personal life, too, Einstein embraced his individuality. He was known for his pacifism, his advocacy for civil rights, and his outspoken views on social and political issues. His willingness to advocate for his beliefs—even when they were unpopular—demonstrated his commitment to living authentically. In many ways, Einstein's legacy is a testament to the power of embracing one's unique perspective in the face of pressures to conform.

Capitalizing on your unique traits, practicing authentic self-expression, and becoming comfortable with deviating from the norm don't just bring success; they validate your inner sense of self-worth, telling you that you're valuable. Embracing your differences encourages you to grow as an individual, and allowing yourself to be an outlier frees you from the weight of social expectations. Owning all parts of who you are pushes you to explore new aspects of your identity, develop new skills, and gain a deeper understanding of how your mind truly works.

Deviating from the norm can be daunting. It's human nature to want to conform, and being different can make you feel vulnerable. Fears of judgment and rejection often deter people from embracing their uniqueness. But developing the courage to do something different is a critical step toward letting go of self-doubt.

Choosing to do something different requires you to embrace uncertainty and view the unknown as a space for growth and discovery. It prompts you to transform fear into excitement, allowing you to see new possibilities. It requires you to persevere in the face of criticism and rejection, using these reactions as feedback and as opportunities to support yourself from within and to exercise your resilience.

This ability to see rejection as a natural part of the growth process lets you build a stronger internal self that cares less about arbitrary norms and social ideals. Choosing to do something different requires you to take control of your own narrative rather than letting someone else dictate it for you. This empowerment leads to a greater sense of agency and autonomy. It allows you to develop a strong sense of self-assurance and to own that your uniqueness is your greatest strength. It fosters a deep, authentic, unshakeable confidence.

TURNING WEAKNESSES INTO STRENGTHS

Sometimes, core parts of who you are can feel like weaknesses when they don't align with a social ideal. Your introversion might be stereotyped as inferior, or a hobby you like might be stigmatized as weird. When you become aware of these social attitudes, it's easy to internalize them to the point that they make you feel inadequate as a person and ashamed of your individuality. This internalization of negative feedback can create self-doubt.

Many cultures prize extroversion, equating verbosity with likability and assertiveness with competence. Because introverts tend to lean on the quieter side, shying away from attention, they often get overlooked in school and the workplace as people assume they lack high-quality ideas. It's common for introverts to start questioning their own worth and competence after enduring enough of these instances. As a result, they may start to feel ashamed of their introversion and view it as a weakness.

When people perceive their introversion as a weakness, they overlook the ways in which it's a hidden strength. Cases in point:

- Introverts have a natural disposition to reflect inward, cultivating a rich inner dialogue that often makes them profound and insightful thinkers. This deep thinking can lead to creative problem-solving and innovative ideas that might not occur to those whose minds are more externally focused.
- Introverts tend to be exceptional listeners. They pay close

attention to the words and emotions of others, offering thoughtful and considered responses. This ability to listen deeply and respond with empathy makes introverts valuable friends and colleagues.

- Introverts are naturally more self-aware, enabling them to understand their motivations, strengths, and areas for personal growth with remarkable clarity. This self-awareness fosters emotional intelligence, allowing them to recognize patterns in their thoughts and behaviors, identify areas for improvement, and make intentional changes. In a world that pushes people to stay busy and distracted, introverts possess the powerful ability to pause, reflect, and grow from within.
- Introverts tend to be emotionally sensitive, which society loves to label as a weakness. If you've ever been told you're too sensitive, it's natural to view your sensitivity as a flaw. However, this sensitivity is a profound strength. Their higher emotional sensitivity means introverts are more attuned to their own feelings, allowing them to process emotions deeply and authentically. This internal attunement makes them highly empathic toward others. Their empathic nature makes many introverts compassionate and nurturing, traits that are highly valued in personal and professional relationships. Sensitivity and empathy are two sides of the same coin; together, they create a powerful tool for building meaningful connections and fostering understanding in any social setting.

Unfortunately, introversion can feel like a weakness despite the strengths it offers, simply because social and cultural norms depict it as different from an ideal. And this stigma doesn't stop at introversion.

Most of your perceived weaknesses aren't actually weaknesses after all; they're *differences*—and they're what you make of them.

When you notice things about yourself that you view as weaknesses, you can find the power in those qualities by reframing them as strengths. Reframing involves changing the way you think about something by viewing it from a different perspective. Instead of viewing your weaknesses from the perspective of other people or of society, challenge yourself to view them from your own personal perspective—your true, genuine perspective—separate from what anyone else thinks. Give your weaknesses the benefit of the doubt and look for the positive abilities they grant you.

For example, if you see yourself as "too quiet," reframe that as being thoughtful and observant—you're someone who listens deeply before speaking. If you feel "too emotional," consider that your emotional depth allows you to connect with others in a meaningful, empathic way. Even traits like overthinking can be reframed as careful analysis or a desire to make well-informed decisions. Struggle with anxiety? That hyper-awareness may help you anticipate problems and prepare for challenges. Have ADHD? Your energy and divergent thinking can fuel bursts of creativity and unconventional problem-solving. Been through a lot of rejection? Those hard experiences have probably strengthened your resilience in the face of adversity. The very qualities you've been taught to downplay may, from a different angle, be your greatest assets.

The very qualities you downplay may, from a different angle, be your greatest assets.

In my life, having cerebral palsy has often felt like a weakness because I'm naturally focused on what it prevents me from doing. In these moments, I'm neglecting a rich flipside of this coin. It's because I've lived my whole life with cerebral palsy that I've developed the resilience to persevere through challenges. It's because of cerebral palsy that I've honed my creative problem-solving skills and figured out my own way of doing things. It's because of cerebral palsy that I've cultivated a growth mindset, always working to improve myself and believing in the capacity for progress. Navigating a world that isn't always accessible to me has created temporary moments of frustration and self-doubt, but it's made me more adaptable and resourceful in the long run.

When you reframe your weaknesses and see them from a clearer point of view, you can embrace them authentically and leverage their power. You can feel more comfortable in who you are rather than doubting your abilities simply because you feel different.

CONFIDENCE, DISTILLED

Resist the Pressure to Conform. Stay true to yourself and resist conforming to societal expectations when they don't feel authentic to who you are.

Celebrate Your Differences. Your unique experiences and challenges give you a distinct and valuable perspective in life. Cherish that.

Capitalize on Your Strengths. Identify your natural talents and strengths and find ways to use them to your advantage.

Reframe Weaknesses as Strengths. Transform perceived weaknesses into strengths by embracing your individuality. By thinking outside the box, you can turn your differences into powerful assets.

Chapter 2

OWN YOUR STRUGGLE, OWN YOUR STORY

My first Valentine's Day in Los Angeles was unforgettable. It was a cool February evening, and the city felt alive with the buzz of romance. I spent the evening with a lovely woman I'd recently started dating. From our first date, our chemistry crackled—an electric connection that felt almost magical.

That evening, she welcomed me into her cozy apartment in West LA. The living room was warmly lit, and the soft hum of jazz music filled the air, creating a perfect ambiance. We indulged in an array of snacks, laughed at each other's stories, and played with her adorable cat, Tira, who seemed to enjoy our company as much as we enjoyed each other's.

As the evening progressed, we nestled into the couch, wrapped in each other's arms. The warmth of her body against mine brought a sense of calm, and—in that moment—it was as if the world outside had ceased to exist. My mind was free from any worry and, for a while, I forgot that I had any kind of disability.

We lay there in silence, enjoying the presence of each other. As her hand rested gently on my chest, I felt my body relax into hers. Then, with a thoughtful and concerned look, she turned to me and asked, "Is everything okay? You're shaking a lot."

Her words brought me back to reality. I hadn't realized it, but my body was shaking like silverware during an earthquake. Constant tremors are one of the plagues of my cerebral palsy. My whole life, I've never known what it's like to sit still, to be in a body whose muscles don't tremor at all times, or to exist in a body that feels at ease with itself. No matter how calm my mind is, my body continues to quiver.

I explained to her that cerebral palsy brings me dystonia, a neurological disorder that causes my muscles to contract involuntarily and tremor. Stillness isn't within reach for me; constant tremor is inescapable. She listened with compassion and understanding, her concern turning into a gentle acceptance that made me feel seen and cared for.

That night, as we continued to cuddle on the couch, I realized that moments of connection and understanding like this are what make life truly meaningful. It reminded me that it's okay to be vulnerable and share the parts of myself I sometimes wish I could hide. I realized it's okay to accept the painful side of my circumstances, to acknowledge my struggles, and to seek comfort in the compassion of others.

It's okay to be vulnerable and share the parts of yourself you want to hide.

I AM WHO I AM—STRUGGLES AND ALL

Cerebral palsy can be a drag. My nervous system is permanently damaged in a way that makes it impossible for me to ever truly relax or sit still. Often, when I'm sitting, I think I'm getting a call because I feel my phone vibrating in my pocket. About half the time, it's not my phone vibrating; it's my thigh vibrating. My thigh is having such a powerful muscle spasm that I can't tell the difference between the tremor of my body and the vibration of my phone. On multiple occasions, I've *missed* calls because I honestly assumed the vibration I felt was just my body doing its thing. Yikes.

When I get out of bed each morning, I know there will be at least one moment ahead when I wish I could escape my body. All day, every day, I experience the kind of tremors that most people only get from a jump scare, panic attack, or caffeine overdose. Muscle tremors make each day of my life feel like I'm locked up in a prison of my own central nervous system. These tremors are just one of the afflictions that define my daily experience. From head to toe, I constantly feel my muscles too tight or too weak, too sore or too floppy, too awkward or too uncoordinated.

I know from my training in psychology that the mind and body are a package deal—inseparable from each other. Neural activity in your brain controls the way your muscles move, how your heart beats, and even what type of personality you have. The lifestyle you live and what you do every day, in turn, shape your brain's neural activity and neurochemistry.

The mind and body are as intertwined as a couple dancing the tango: Each partner is attuned to the other's movements, creating a fluid and coordinated performance that only comes alive from the interaction between both parties. My physical suffering is part of my body's hardwiring, and it's as fundamental to who I am as my personality, my laugh, or my smile. To seek an escape from my body would be to deny my real sense of self in pursuit of an unattainable illusion.

I am who I am, with my abilities and my limitations. At times, I feel like cerebral palsy is a curse, an invisible weight I carry every day. That feeling can bring about a negative knee-jerk reaction where I imagine myself without any disability and focus on hiding my limitations so I can pretend they don't exist. As natural as this reaction is, I don't think it's a very good one. It's a rejection of who I am now and who I always will be.

Rather than living in fantasy land, I prefer a different path: accepting that my struggles are a real part of me. I choose to be an empowered victim of my situation by embracing my limitations and finding strength in my vulnerability.

WHEN BEING THE VICTIM IS EMPOWERING

Wait, what? You choose to be a victim? Yes, you read that right. And I get it—by and large, people say it's bad to view yourself as the victim. They assume that identifying as a victim means making excuses, assigning blame to others, and giving up a sense of control over your life. The common belief is that viewing yourself as a victim strips away your power and agency. However, I think this perspective oversimplifies the complex psychology of victimhood, overlooking its potential to be an empowering source of confidence.

There is no shame or weakness in acknowledging yourself as a victim of your circumstances. In fact, recognizing your victimhood can be a form of self-care—a vital step toward self-love, self-acceptance, and personal growth. It's about accepting your struggles as they truly are and offering yourself the compassion you deserve. It's about understanding that the challenges you face are legitimate and not always within your control. It's about releasing self-blame and fully embracing the truth that *your struggles are not your fault.*

Sometimes the most compassionate thing you can do for yourself is to admit the truth: This is hard.

A healthy victim identity is vastly different from the toxic victim mentality most people are familiar with. Some individuals adopt a victim mindset to create distorted narratives about their lives, viewing themselves as powerless so they can avoid accountability and the need to change. This is very bad. Giving up on your own ability to influence your fate is not a form of self-love or compassion; it's a form of self-abandonment and it's an unhealthy mentality. It involves abandoning your sense of agency, which prevents you from feeling confident, content, or capable.

Healthy victimhood, meanwhile, is nuanced and balanced. It means accepting your struggles as legitimate and recognizing that they're not always your fault. At the same time, it acknowledges your power to shape your future. This balanced perspective allows you to operate with a sense of self-compassion *and* agency.

By accepting that many aspects of life are beyond your control, you can stop blaming yourself for your struggles. Conversely, by recognizing that other aspects *are* within your control, you can take accountability and understand that you have the power to write your life story from today onward. Embracing this duality means accepting that you can be both a victim and a hero at the same time, making the most of your circumstances.

Introverts whose inner voices echo loudly need to hear this more than anyone: Don't beat yourself up for things that aren't your fault. Unproductive self-criticism is not the same as healthy self-reflection. Embrace your inner experiences, but don't let them trap you in a cycle of helplessness. Use your reflective nature to understand your challenges, grant yourself compassion, and then seek ways to overcome them.

VICTIMS BECOME HEROES OF THEMSELVES

Seeing yourself as a victim doesn't take away your ability to be your own hero. In fact, it encourages it. The most confident people are those who understand and accept their losses in life, coming to terms with the ways they've suffered. They process their losses and grant themselves the compassion they need to heal and move on. They don't blame themselves for the adversities they face due to chance, but they hold themselves accountable for working through their issues as best they can. They know that it's up to them to define their own goals and plans from here on, taking their lives into their own hands with a sense of agency and control over their fate. They accept their victimhood while stepping into their heroism.

Being a victim of your circumstances doesn't erase your power to be the hero of your story.

It takes vulnerability and courage to settle into this healthy balance of victim-hero identity. The dual identity of being both a victim and a hero at the same time isn't a radical concept; it's a normal part of being human. But when the fear of vulnerability stands in the way, embracing this duality is a challenge. Vulnerability may seem like something you just express to the outer world—those times when you open up to others. Yet vulnerability is also a way you reflect inward on yourself. It's when you recognize, understand, and accept all parts of yourself.

The healthiest kinds of self-reflections are nuanced; they acknowledge a variety of aspects within you, even those that seem at odds with one another. The hard truth? Humans are complicated. Very complicated. And we need to appreciate that complexity.

When you reflect on yourself with vulnerability, you acknowledge ways in which you're both a victim and a hero, even if these two labels seem contradictory. You see both of these identities as true parts of your broader sense of self, setting your mind up for authentic, self-accepting confidence. Barriers to confidence emerge when your self-reflections acknowledge only one of those parts, like if you reflect on only your victim or hero side without noting the other. That paints a biased picture.

SELF-REFLECTIONS TELL A STORY

When people acknowledge only their victim identity or hero identity while denying the other, they don't just lose touch with a core part of themselves; they also misinterpret the part of themselves they feel in touch with. Embracing both victimhood and heroism creates a coherent story arc in your mind and provides perspective. It allows you to contextualize your pain and triumph within each other, maintaining a balanced viewpoint and a healthy sense of confidence. Denying one element of this duality disrupts this balance.

Acknowledging only your victim identity causes your mind to exaggerate negative events, pushing you deeper into a mentality of helplessness. Viewing yourself as a victim, and *only* a victim, makes you feel like crap. These "victim-based reflections" are critical self-judgments. They threaten your confidence because they tell stories of your suffering while denying you any personal agency to do anything about it.

Suppose you go out on a date and have a great time, but the other person isn't interested in seeing you again. This rejection could lead you to tell yourself, "I'm unlovable" or "I'm unattractive," as you feel bad for yourself and imagine a lifetime of loneliness. Or suppose you're giving a presentation at work, and in the middle of presenting to your boss and coworkers, you find yourself nervous and thinking, "I'm not smart enough for this job" or "I shouldn't have just said that," as you wallow in self-pity.

These judgments are forms of self-doubt that paint yourself as a helpless victim suffering at the expense of the world, without the ability to change anything. They embody the classic victim mentality that wise people advise against, as they involve abandoning yourself, doubting your worth, and denying your ability to influence your fate. These victim-based reflections carry a voice that says, "Everything sucks, and it always will suck."

Avoid falling into this mental hole at all costs.

Then there are pure hero-based reflections. Just as victim-based reflections are toxically negative on their own, hero-based reflections without an awareness of victimhood are toxically positive and tenuous. They proclaim, "Everything is great, it always has been great, and it always will be great."

At face value, hero-based reflections sound good. They project an image of confidence and provide a feeling to match. However, the problem is that hero-based reflections give people a one-sided worldview that denies reality and is easily threatened. The confidence these reflections give isn't stable, genuine, or reliable. When you rely solely on hero-based reflections, you deny any suffering you've experienced in life, prevent yourself from processing trauma or adversity, and thus hold yourself back from building resilience. You feel threatened by the slightest sign of despair and are never fully at ease in your own skin, even if you achieve great feats with a sense of audacity.

When people refuse to see themselves as a victim, it's usually because they think that victim and hero identities are mutually exclusive—they're either one or the other, not both—and, when given a choice, they'd rather be the hero. This type of one-sided, black-and-white thinking is a common cognitive error people make in all areas of life, and it inevitably causes people to jump to conclusions and ignore important parts of reality. It's a problematic instinct you need to work on overriding.

Seeing yourself as both the victim *and* the hero of your life story is empowering because it stops your mind from oversimplifying your situation into a dichotomy. It supports self-acceptance across the full spectrum of who you are. It allows you to develop more confidence by having compassion for your struggles while believing in your ability to determine your own fate. You can see your situation for what it truly is, without falsely forcing it to fit into a purely victim or purely hero narrative—neither of which on their own will ever capture reality with 100 percent accuracy. The confidence this way of thinking brings is authentic, stable, and powerful.

Accepting the full weight of your struggle is the first step to lifting it.

THE POWER OF ATTRIBUTIONS

One of my favorite psychological theories is called attribution theory. Studying it has helped me understand how my mind works in ways I hadn't realized before. It's enabled me to see how I sometimes blame myself for difficulties in my life, preventing me from giving myself the compassion I need. This self-insight has helped me develop confidence by taking control over my mind's attributions.

Attribution theory describes how people explain the causes of events and behaviors in life. It helps us understand whether we attribute our experiences to internal factors, like our own abilities, or to external factors, like the environment around us. It's how we tie anything we observe in the world to an underlying cause, making sense of the things we see. Here's an example:

Imagine you're walking around a mall. You see clothing stores to your left, tech stores to your right, and a food court ahead. As you keep walking, you notice a man on your right kicking and shaking a vending machine, screaming loudly and angrily, "Come on!"

What do you make of this scene?

According to attribution theory, there are a variety of ways you might explain why this man is acting the way he is. Attribution theory suggests that even though you're not entirely sure what's brought about this man's behavior, you'll likely make a quick guess—a snap judgment of attribution—to sort things out in your own head.

One common attribution is to view people as responsible for their behavior. This is usually the simplest and easiest explanation. When we do this, we make character judgments about others. For example, we might make sense of this scene at the mall by concluding that this man has anger management issues and is short-tempered. We might even just conclude that he's a bad person.

An alternative attribution is to view someone's environment as responsible for their behavior. Instead of assuming that this man's behavior says anything about his personality, you might focus on the situation or context he's in. For example, you might think about the vending machine as a likely cause of the man's behavior. This external focus encourages you to give this man the benefit of the doubt, assuming that the vending machine was malfunctioning and not giving him the snack he rightfully paid for. When you take this external focus, you don't judge this man as an ill-tempered jerk. Rather, you have empathy and compassion for him, understanding that you, too, might act the same way if you were in that situation, dealing with a broken vending machine that just ate your last dollar bill. And if you've indeed been in that kind of situation before, you know exactly what it feels like—and how that feeling can hijack your behavior.

Life is complicated, and we really don't know why some things around us happen as they do. Because the human mind hates ambiguity, it's quick to form attributions, making up a story about what just happened and why it happened. We instinctively attribute feelings, behaviors, and events in our lives to underlying causes, focusing a great deal of our attention and judgment on those imagined causes. Our minds automatically—and without our awareness—create an imagined cause and plotline for our current situation, treating that cause as fact and that plotline as inevitable destiny. As comforting and easy as this way of thinking might be, it often steers us astray.

RETHINKING YOUR ATTRIBUTIONS

When people see themselves as either a victim or hero—but not both—they're making a one-sided attribution. They're interpreting events in their lives by focusing on only part of a full story because that simple one-sided story is easier to understand. This one-sidedness is why victim and hero identities on their own are problematic. They stem from instinctive attributions that are biased and false, yet your mind favors them for their simplicity. When left unmonitored, the mind tends to prefer simplicity over accuracy.

It's crucial to become aware of your attributions and question whether they're serving you or holding you back. The issue with many instinctive attributions is that they choose their side based on the unresolved inner turmoil that lies deep within your mind. Your insecurities, ego, past traumas, and anxieties bias your mind to favor certain attributions over others. As a result, the stories you tell yourself about your life may really be biased manifestations of your subconscious mind—not accurate realities. Often, it's best to pause for a moment and rethink them.

In my own life, rethinking the attributions I make about my physical abilities has enabled me to see myself as both a victim and a hero of my story. In turn, it has allowed me to develop more confidence from an authentic and vulnerable place, accepting myself with greater clarity.

When evaluating children with cerebral palsy, doctors often classify the severity of the child's condition as either mild, moderate, or severe. Growing up, I was always told I had mild cerebral palsy—just mild, nothing too impactful—which felt true when I compared myself to other people with cerebral palsy who needed help feeding, bathing, and dressing themselves.

As a child, it felt empowering to define myself as having only a mild disability. It allowed me to disidentify with my differences and feel more like my peers. It also made me work hard at achieving everything my classmates or older brothers did, because I felt anything they could do was within my reach too, as long as I put in the effort. But no matter how hard I worked, there were certain things I still struggled with and physical challenges I could not overcome.

Experiencing awful pain in my hands each day at school as I struggled to take notes in class didn't feel like a *mild* impairment. Having to be pushed around in a stroller as a ten-year-old kid because I couldn't walk far didn't feel *mild.* And the inescapable pain of each muscle tremor throughout my body all day and night? That didn't feel *mild.*

I viewed myself as having only a mild disability, yet I felt restricted and was suffering in heavy ways. Believing I had mild cerebral palsy made me downplay my disability. It made me doubt the legitimacy of my limitations and deny myself the intensity of the struggles I faced. Unable to attribute my hardships to the severity of my disability, I instead attributed many of my inabilities to my lack of will or effort. Thinking my cerebral palsy was only mild, I figured that all these problems couldn't possibly be because of my disability—surely, *I* had to be the problem.

Shifts in my attributions began in places as simple as a piano bench. One day, as a child, I sat down determined to teach myself a simple song. I knew the notes in my head, but my fingers wouldn't move the way I wanted. In that moment, everything clicked: This wasn't about willpower—it was about the physical realities of my condition. Some struggles weren't weaknesses I could conquer by trying harder; they were walls I'd been punching my whole life. Only by recognizing my disability as more severe, and accepting that reality, did I shift my attributions and allow my mind to tell me: *I'm doing all that I can.* That reframing helped me meet myself with compassion, let go of self-blame, and quiet my self-doubt.

Acknowledging the true severity of any condition or circumstance you face in life is a form of self-care. By recognizing the weight of a matter for all that it is, you allow yourself to see your struggles as valid and any progress you make as significant. Denying the severity of a condition can feel empowering in the moment, but it can set unrealistic expectations that invalidate the legitimacy of your struggles.

Acknowledging your struggles isn't weakness. It's self-respect.

As an adult, I've accepted that my disability isn't mild. But I also recognize that this doesn't mean I'm unable to challenge my limits and achieve great things. This acceptance makes me proud of myself for all that I have set out to do, persevered through, and ultimately accomplished. It makes me feel compassion for myself when I struggle and reminds me that I define success for myself in a way that's unique to me, not in comparison to others. It makes me accept myself as a victim of a brain injury and a hero of my life since.

It's empowering to rethink the attributions you make about your life with a kinder eye toward your struggles. Maintaining a growth mindset and a sense of agency over the way you live allows you to accept that you're the victim of things out of your control while becoming the hero of the things you *can* control. Validating your struggles as legitimate while believing in your ability to pave your own path is a key step toward developing authentic, resilient, and lasting confidence.

CONFIDENCE, DISTILLED

Your Struggles Are Legitimate. Recognize and accept that your challenges are real and valid. This acknowledgment is essential for practicing self-compassion.

Victimhood Can Be Empowering. It's okay to feel like a victim of circumstances beyond your control. Acknowledging victimhood can be a powerful act of self-love and self-acceptance.

Embrace Both Victim and Hero Identities. Recognize that being a victim doesn't diminish your capacity to be the hero of your story. Acknowledge your struggles while also believing in your power to overcome adversity and shape your future.

Chapter 3

STEPPING INTO VULNERABILITY

A few years ago, I had the honor of attending my friend's stand-up comedy debut. His five-minute set was tucked into a three-hour show at a venue an hour's drive from my home. It was quite an ordeal just to see those five minutes, but I didn't hesitate for a moment. I was thrilled to watch him perform.

Parched from my long drive, I eagerly ordered a bottle of water as the show began. When the server brought my drink, I knew I was in for a challenge. It was one of those glass bottles with an absurdly tight cap. My worst enemy.

I have a long, complicated history with water bottles—and all kinds of drink containers, for that matter. Cerebral palsy lets my hands function about as well as a toddler's, so handling anything other than a pre-poured cup is a struggle. Eyeing this glass bottle, I stretched out my hands, took a few deep breaths, and mentally prepared for battle. I was thirsty and I was determined to conquer this cap, no matter what it took.

As it turns out, it took a lot from me.

Three comedians came and went onstage while I sat in my seat, investing every ounce of mental and physical strength I had trying to open that bottle. I wrestled it with both hands for fifteen minutes, attacking that screw-on cap as if it held a rare treasure inside, doing anything I could to yank it open. All to no avail.

Now covered in sweat, exhausted, and boiling with frustration, I looked around to see other audience members effortlessly sipping their drinks. The guy sitting next to me, who had ordered the same water bottle, snapped his cap off in a second. Did I ask him for help opening mine? Of course not. I'd rather have stayed thirsty for three hours than make undue conversation with a random stranger about my disability—and so, that's exactly what I did that night. Parched *and* proud.

As the night went on, my friend finally took the stage. Watching him perform his set was both inspiring and humbling. Despite his nerves, he embraced his debut with full zeal. He put himself out there despite the fear of failure or embarrassment. His performance reminded me that everyone, regardless of their circumstances, battles vulnerability. His courage and determination let me see once more that vulnerability isn't a sign of weakness; it's a sign of strength and a testament to your humanity.

Vulnerability isn't weakness—it's a sign of strength and a testament to your humanity.

For me, the crux of vulnerability is asking for help. Admitting I need help with anything related to my disability makes my insides crumple like paper. My desire to feel capable even makes me deny my disability to myself. Acknowledging my cerebral palsy can feel like admitting weakness, exposing my deepest flaws and struggles, and labeling myself as less than.

My reluctance to ask for help with that water bottle wasn't just about the bottle. It symbolized my struggle to accept and be open about my limitations. In trying to prove my capability, I isolated myself from the support that could help me flourish.

Vulnerability isn't about defeat; it's about embracing the full spectrum of the human experience, including your need for connection and support. For introverts especially, this often means summoning the courage to step out of your comfort zone, choosing connection over solitude in times of hardship. It means reaching out for help and support rather than fighting your battles alone. Even when vulnerability feels like a betrayal of your natural instincts, it's often a crucial path toward greater self-understanding, deeper connections, and celebrating yourself more fully.

TO BE OR NOT TO BE VULNERABLE

At that comedy show, I never asked for help opening my water bottle. I didn't ask the server, the guy next to me, or any of the comedians onstage (who probably would have appreciated the impromptu comedic material). Instead, I decided that enduring three hours of dehydration was easier than asking for help when I needed it.

This reaction is perfectly normal. In fact, it's a basic instinct. Steering clear of vulnerability a natural psychological defense mechanism that keeps you feeling safe. It feels *comfortable*. Vulnerability emerges when your fears, doubts, and insecurities surface—parts of yourself you prefer to keep hidden. Sometimes, you might even deny these parts of yourself exist at all. Being vulnerable means exposing a raw version of yourself and letting your guard down. It can be scary because it involves showing your true self, including your imperfections and struggles. It means admitting you need help, even when that feels like a threat to your self-image.

Yet vulnerability is about so much more than asking for help. It's saying, "No." Saying, "I love you." Admitting fear. Asking for forgiveness. It's apologizing to your child. Raising your hand to ask a "stupid" question. Saying, "I'm not okay," when someone asks how you are. It's applying for a job you might not get. It's speaking up in a meeting when your voice is shaking. It's letting someone see you cry.

While avoiding vulnerability is normal, that doesn't mean it's healthy. Embracing vulnerability is a powerful strength. To be vulnerable is an act of bravery and profound trust. It takes great courage and effort, but it allows you to connect genuinely with others, receive the support you need, and let the rawest parts of yourself feel less burdensome and more understood.

By allowing yourself to be vulnerable, you embrace the full spectrum of the human experience. You acknowledge that it's okay to have limitations. You recognize that opening up to the world is not a sign of weakness but a testament to your resilience and authenticity, and one of the most powerful forms of self-care. By being open about your struggles, you invite others into your journey and create opportunities for deeper understanding and acceptance—not just in letting others accept you, but in allowing you to accept yourself.

THE VULNERABILITY EQUILIBRIUM

Reflect on your own struggles and limitations. What types of experiences make you feel most vulnerable and exposed to the world? In what ways do you avoid those experiences, and when do you allow—or even *want*—yourself to feel vulnerable?

Vulnerability is a dance. It's a back-and-forth movement each one of us navigates throughout life, allowing us to find our ideal balance between exposure and concealment—our vulnerability equilibrium. Here's how the vulnerability equilibrium works:

When you're too vulnerable with others, you risk putting your emotional well-being into their hands instead of your own. You cross healthy boundaries, disclose excessively, and open yourself up to unnecessary harm.

When you're not vulnerable enough, you isolate yourself psychologically and hold yourself back from growing fully, feeling deeply, and living expansively. You deny your authenticity, miss out on opportunities for deeper social connections, and lose a key part of what makes you . . . you.

Navigating the vulnerability equilibrium by settling into a healthy level of vulnerability is a key step toward developing true confidence. It isn't one you can skip. Without balancing unrestrained vulnerability with selective self-protection, you can never feel fully comfortable in your own skin. A healthy sense of vulnerability means understanding, accepting, and openly sharing your struggles thoughtfully and appropriately, given the time and place. It also means knowing how to regulate your emotional pains without dumping them onto others.

Healthy vulnerability makes you more comfortable with who you are and makes others feel more comfortable with you. It fosters deeper self-awareness, as well as empathy and compassion from those who know you.

Vulnerability helps you feel comfortable with who you are—and makes others feel comfortable with you too.

To me, healthy vulnerability is one of the greatest signs of psychological strength. It signals a strong internal compass. The reality of being vulnerable is that you open yourself up to the possibility of others harming you. In vulnerable moments, you may feel emotionally raw and hypersensitive. Others' words can wield a sharp edge, just as glances, gestures, and even the smallest facial expressions can. Any inkling that you're inadequate can feel threatening, whether it's real or imagined. But a healthy sense of vulnerability means grounding yourself in your own truth, setting your own course, and being true to your internal compass. It means knowing that nothing anyone else feels about you can change the way you feel about yourself.

When you act from a vulnerability equilibrium, moments of vulnerability no longer seem so scary. In fact, they might just be nuggets of beauty that make life worth living.

FINDING YOUR VULNERABILITY EQUILIBRIUM

When I was a freshman in high school, a friend on the school newspaper wanted to write a feature about my life with cerebral palsy. He believed my story could raise awareness for students with disabilities. I was naturally intrigued by the idea of being featured in the newspaper and gaining attention from my peers. It sounded like a pretty cool gig. The only issue was, while my close friends were aware I had cerebral palsy, it wasn't something I liked discussing with other classmates—let alone the entire 1,300-student school.

Despite my wariness, I decided to go forward with the story. I shared my struggles from early childhood, my experience learning to play table tennis, and the things I still felt limited by as a teenager. The story was as raw and vulnerable as it could possibly have been. The night before the story launched, I was filled with fears: *Would people start treating me differently? Would they pester me with questions about my disability? Would they suddenly start asking me if I needed help all the time?*

At this point in my life, I hadn't had many experiences being truly vulnerable. I felt I was putting myself at risk emotionally by sharing my deepest insecurities with the entire school, placing my self-esteem in their hands.

The day the story came out, people all over school came up to me with high fives, fist pumps, and kind words. Classmates—and even teachers—I'd never met before told me they liked the feature and found my story inspirational. Some even wanted to challenge me in table tennis. People seemed to feel an emotional closeness with me, and I felt a connection to them in return. I didn't feel exposed; I felt seen.

The support I received that day filled me with a tremendous sense of acceptance, helping me embrace more of myself. The experience boosted my confidence and revealed the power of vulnerability. It marked the beginning of my journey to find my vulnerability equilibrium.

Before that experience, I'd resisted opening up. Since then, I've learned when and with whom to disclose my cerebral palsy so that moments of vulnerability enhance my connections, authenticity, and comfort. Not every time and place is right for vulnerability. On a first date, you shouldn't spill your trauma. At work, you shouldn't give your boss a play-by-play of your worst breakup. That's not real vulnerability; that's oversharing. And the sad reality is that not every person is worth trusting with your truth. Some people won't accept or respect you. Even in the right time and place, self-disclosure can carry serious risks.

Knowing when to be vulnerable and when to keep certain things to yourself takes practice. It requires experience to sense the level of emotional safety in a space and to know whether you can trust those in whom you're confiding. The more you find your vulnerability equilibrium, the more you can live openly, safely, and authentically. The more you can connect with others—and with yourself.

VULNERABILITY CONNECTS AND HEALS

The mind has an intriguing duality. It has an inner self you perceive as your true identity and an outer self you present to the world. The more closely these two selves align, the more authentic and confident you'll feel. For introverts, who tend to have a more pronounced sense of inner self than outer self, achieving this alignment can be particularly challenging but it's also crucial.

People who resist vulnerability prevent their inner and outer selves from aligning. They're well aware of their inner monologue—the voice inside their head that tells them how they truly feel about themselves—but they impose a strong filter on it. They don't feel comfortable sharing their insecurities, struggles, or anxieties with others, so they keep these negative thoughts locked up inside. Several common beliefs drive this behavior, sounding something like this: "It's scary," "I'll be seen as weak," or "Other people don't want to hear my issues." It's perfectly normal to experience these thoughts and fear vulnerability. But it's not healthy to let those fears control your mind and behavior.

Resisting vulnerability doesn't just deny your ability to accept and express yourself. It also hurts your relationships. When you hide your insecurities, fears, and limitations from others, even your closest friendships and intimate relationships can have an underlying hollowness to them. Without vulnerability, relationships can lack deep trust, acceptance, and a sense of unconditional support—enablers of self-confidence you gain from a healthy social life.

Being vulnerable earns others' respect, empathy, and appreciation for your perspective. Most people instinctively respond to vulnerability with care, compassion, and validation. Vulnerable moments are often surprisingly positive because they humanize and normalize struggle. Plus, vulnerability is contagious: When you open up to others, they're more likely to do the same to you. Brené Brown, a leading researcher on vulnerability, highlights that vulnerability is the birthplace of love, belonging, joy, courage, empathy, and creativity. She explains that when we share our vulnerabilities, we create a space where others feel safe to share theirs too. This mutual openness fosters trust and mutual support that benefits everyone. Vulnerability begets vulnerability, creating deeply meaningful social connections that go both ways.

Being vulnerable and receiving compassion primes your mind for confidence. It validates your self-worth, reinforces your ability to belong and be loved, and makes you feel accepted. It lightens self-doubts and lessens insecurities. By acknowledging and sharing your vulnerabilities, you begin to accept yourself more fully from within. When you feel accepted for the full spectrum of who you are, you feel less worried about concealing certain parts of yourself from the world. You no longer feel the need to divide your inner and outer selves. Your filter starts to dissipate, empowering you to live more authentically with a unified sense of identity.

Even when vulnerable moments don't bring compassion from others, they still develop your confidence by building resilience, self-insight, and self-care. Just as feeling accepted and supported bring confidence, so can rejection and criticism. While painful in the moment, rejection and criticism are valuable in the long run because we can learn from them.

Facing and expressing your vulnerabilities strengthens your ability to handle difficult emotions and situations, promoting personal growth and deepening resilience over time. By embracing vulnerability, you learn to navigate discomfort and uncertainty more effectively, allowing yourself to bounce back from future setbacks and challenges with greater ease. You learn to believe in yourself.

Each time you step into vulnerability, it makes you stronger. When you receive negative feedback from others, you can show yourself the care you'd give to someone else in your shoes. You can prove to yourself that you can endure the discomfort of vulnerability and move onward, letting the fear of that discomfort hold you back less. You can take pride in having had the strength to be vulnerable. You can know that the more vulnerable

The more you allow yourself to be vulnerable, the less scary vulnerability becomes.

experiences you get through, the less fear your mind ultimately attaches to those experiences.

When you replace fear with self-pride, your confidence in handling future vulnerable situations grows. You realize that the power of vulnerability lies in your own inner monologue, not in the feedback you get from others. Others' feedback is merely a precursor to your inner voice; it has no weight on its own. It only has the value you let your mind assign to it.

As you step into your vulnerability equilibrium, you reduce the emotional burden of hiding your true self, lifting from your shoulders any feelings of shame, guilt, or isolation that can weigh you down. When you're no longer held back by the fear of appearing weak, you feel more comfortable putting yourself out there. This nurtures your confidence further, creating a positive feedback loop: Confidence enables vulnerability, which in turn builds more confidence.

STEPPING INTO YOUR VULNERABILITY

The best way to become more comfortable with vulnerability is to start with small acts of opening up. Share a fuller spectrum of your experiences with those you trust, allowing them to see both your highs and your lows.

Begin by sharing small, everyday vulnerabilities with trusted friends, colleagues, or family. This might include admitting that you don't understand a topic in a conversation or expressing a minor personal concern. Start small. For example, if you feel anxious before a presentation, share this with a colleague or friend. This simple act of admitting your feelings can reduce your emotional burden and make it easier to handle the situation. It helps you acknowledge, accept, and process your emotions, making you feel less restricted by them. Starting with small issues can build your ability to be open without feeling overwhelmed. As your comfort level grows, take it a step further: Say "no" when it's tough. Apologize when your ego tells you not to. Allow yourself to cry instead of holding back the waterworks.

Seek out empathic and supportive people who can understand your experiences. This might include friends, family, a therapist, a coach, an online community, or members of a support group. Find spaces where you can express yourself without fear of judgment and decide for yourself what you're comfortable sharing and with whom. Being vulnerable doesn't mean sharing everything with everyone; it's important to recognize when and with whom it's appropriate to be vulnerable. Find people who can relate to your feelings and appreciate your vulnerability, holding it with the care it deserves.

Pay attention to any negative thoughts that arise when you consider being vulnerable. You might notice thoughts like "People will judge me," "It's bad to show weakness," or "I don't want to bother them." Identifying these thoughts is the first step toward challenging them. Reframe negative thoughts with more positive and realistic ones. For example, instead of thinking, "People will judge me," reframe it to "Being open can help others relate to me." This shift in perspective can make it easier to practice vulnerability.

Mindfulness practices—such as meditation, deep breathing, or yoga—can also help. If you're afraid of vulnerability, your body will probably tighten up when you try to be vulnerable. It's a physiological reaction. By calming these physical responses, mindfulness helps you stay present, see situations more clearly, and manage the discomfort that comes with opening up. In doing so, it makes vulnerability feel less like a threat and more like a choice. It makes opening yourself up easier.

After each experience of vulnerability, sit with your emotions. Take time to reflect on what you learned and how it made you feel. This reflection can help you understand your growth and settle into your vulnerability equilibrium, planting more seeds of confidence in your mind.

CONFIDENCE, DISTILLED

Vulnerability Is Strength. Embracing vulnerability isn't a sign of weakness; it's a strength that lets you accept who you are and connect with others.

Find Your Vulnerability Equilibrium. Achieve a balance between self-protection and self-disclosure by understanding when it's safe and appropriate to open up, maximizing the benefits of vulnerability.

Vulnerability Brings Authentic Confidence. Allowing yourself to be vulnerable aligns your inner and outer selves, fostering a genuine and lasting sense of confidence.

Chapter 4

IMPROVISE

When I was a PhD student at UCLA, I worked as a teaching assistant for a small psychology class of twenty students. My role was straightforward: help students with assignments, grade papers, and show up to class. Piece of cake. The professor handled the rest. He showed up early, brought the lecture, and led the show. In short? He was Batman and I was Robin.

But one day, midway through the quarter, I strolled absentmindedly into class only to find the professor absent and the room full of students ready to learn. My heart beat a bit faster. *This isn't how things are supposed to work,* I thought. So, I waited, hoping the professor would walk through the door any second.

A minute passed. Then two. Then three. And before I knew it, it was five minutes past the hour, and I had twenty pairs of eyes looking to me for direction. My stomach tightened. I had no clue what the lesson was supposed to be. My plan for the day had been to sit back, open my laptop, and get some of my own work done.

Clearly, that plan was out the window—and Robin would have to become Batman.

Oh crap . . .

Standing in front of the class, I felt both a weakness and a strength. The weakness was obvious: I wasn't prepared to teach, especially not for two full hours. The strength, however, came from an unexpected source: my improv training. As a budding comedian with a few months of improv under my belt, I knew how to work a room and think on my feet. Was an academic classroom really that different from a comedy theater?

I took a deep breath and admitted to the students the core of my fear: I had no idea what the day's lesson was supposed to be. I told them we were in the same boat and that my goal was to give them the best class possible, despite the circumstances. I also promised to be fully open and honest about what I did and didn't know. This moment of humility seemed to resonate with them; they appreciated the candor and the unusual lecture style.

Throughout the class, I figured out a lesson plan bit by bit, adding my own twist to the material, cracking jokes, and engaging with the students as peers. Somehow, the class was a hit. My authenticity and vulnerability turned what could have been a disaster into a lively ordeal, and I embraced the uncertain improvisation of it all with confidence. I didn't freak out or panic, even when I very well could have. Rather, I settled into the uncertainty and trusted the process. My confidence, I realized, made my students feel comfortable and confident too. The energy was high, and several students even stayed after class to chat with me about psychology, graduate school, and life in general. I hadn't just *survived* this chaotic class—I'd crushed it.

That day, I left the classroom with a profound sense of purpose and fulfillment. By embracing the vulnerability of unpreparedness and practicing humility, I stayed confident and created a collaborative space for learning and improvisation. To this day, my impromptu class remains one of my favorite teaching experiences, and I hope it was a positive memory for those students.

THE PERILS OF PLANNING

Rigid planning and preparation can create a false sense of confidence by masking an inner fear of vulnerability. Feeling like you know what to expect in life makes you feel comfortable and capable. When you anticipate challenges and prepare yourself to handle them ahead of time, you can feel confident by feeling in control over your situation. However, control is tenuous and the confidence that comes from it is shaky.

> **Overplanning can mask a fear of vulnerability, giving you only the illusion of confidence.**

The peril of overplanning is that it holds you back from adapting to the unexpected. The real world is unpredictable, and strict planning can hinder your flexibility when things go off script. Life is chaotic, and events rarely unfold exactly as planned. Unpredictable factors—like sudden changes in weather, unexpected technical failures, or even a professor's no-show—can disrupt the most carefully laid plans. Overplanning leaves little room for flexibility.

Grounding your confidence solely in knowing what to expect can be detrimental. When things don't go according to plan, your confidence can easily waver. The solution? Improv.

True confidence comes not just from planning but from the ability to adapt and improvise when faced with the unexpected. This

True confidence comes not just from planning but from the ability to adapt and improvise when faced with the unexpected.

adaptability ensures that you remain resilient and capable, even when things don't go according to plan. Embracing uncertainty and learning to improvise helps you build a more robust and authentic confidence—one that can withstand the unpredictable nature of life.

THE POWER OF IMPROVISATION

When I first started performing stand-up comedy, I meticulously memorized every word of my set, planning each vocal inflection, hand gesture, and pause. I'd walk up onstage with a sense of control and safety, anchoring my confidence in the predictability of a rehearsed script. But when I totally messed up my set's length in the U.S. Comedy Contest, I realized how fragile this approach really is. I'd prepared a five-minute set for a three-minute show, and the moment I discovered this, my confidence evaporated. I became helpless. My carefully crafted routine became useless, and in that moment, I felt completely vulnerable, afraid of failure and embarrassment.

In that moment of crisis, I discovered the power of improvisation. Faced with the choice of withdrawing from the contest or stepping onstage unprepared, I chose the latter. This decision showed me that my confidence didn't have to come solely from rigid preparation; it could come from my ability to accept the present moment and adapt in real time.

Introverts are natural improvisers. Sounds ridiculous, doesn't it? After all, improv is one of the most absurdly loud, outgoing, and performative things a person could possibly do. But hear me out: That image of improv is simply a slice of the full picture. It's the image of an improv *show*, a theatrical production meant for an audience to laugh at.

The full picture of improv is actually one of adaptability, presence, and connection. It's not about performing on a stage; it's about navigating the stage of life. At its core, improv is a way of thinking and being. It's about responding to the unexpected with curiosity instead of fear; building on other people's ideas rather than shutting them down; and listening deeply to others while staying true to yourself. For introverts, these principles come naturally. And guess what? They're the building blocks of self-confidence in social situations.

Improv is a way of thinking and being. It's about responding to the unexpected with curiosity instead of fear; building on other people's ideas rather than shutting them down; and listening deeply to others while staying true to yourself.

Improvisation—not as a theatrical production, but as a way of life—means embracing uncertainty and trusting yourself to navigate the unknown. It requires being present, listening, and responding without a predetermined agenda. When introverts practice improv, they use their listening skills, observational acuity, creativity, intuitions, and thoughtful responses to move *with* the world around them rather than letting it move them. Improv encourages introverts to stay true to themselves rather than trying to fit into a predetermined mold.

In many ways, improv is a simulation of social behavior. Personally, the teachings of improv have made me less anxious, more adaptable, and more comfortable in moments of vulnerability, ultimately making me a more resilient and confident person. They might just do the same for you.

IMPROV LESSONS ARE LIFE LESSONS

Improv is a psychological mudslide where vulnerability and confidence intersect to create something magical. Feeling vulnerable is frightening because it means lowering your defenses and exposing your true self, making you feel like you could be judged or hurt. Planning, meanwhile, serves as a shield against this vulnerability, providing a sense of control and predictability. But improv? It rewrites the unwritten script, forcing your vulnerability to be the very thing that sparks your confidence.

When you improvise, you strip away your ability to plan, revealing your authentic thoughts and behaviors in real time. You force yourself to face your fear of the unknown—the unplanned—throwing away your ability to filter and curate the image you present to the world. For most people, this is terrifying. It's open, raw, and vulnerable. But it's precisely this vulnerability that breeds confidence. Good improvisers are confident not despite their vulnerability but *because* of it. Improv teaches you to stop running away from vulnerability and to start embracing it. And once you do, you trust yourself more. You doubt yourself less. And you find strength in your authenticity, knowing that your in-the-moment intuitions aren't as foolish as you'd thought—in fact, they're wiser than you ever gave them credit for.

I've been studying and performing improv for several years now, and it's taught me truths about human nature that I didn't learn during my PhD in psychology. Through improv, I've identified four common thought processes that hold people back from developing self-confidence in life:

1. The fear of uncertainty
2. Compulsive overthinking
3. The fear of failure
4. Attachment to an agenda

Improv offers practical techniques to overcome each of these four thought processes and boost confidence. Here's how:

Lesson 1: Step into Uncertainty

Life is full of uncertainty, and human behavior is largely unpredictable. No one knows exactly how their day will unfold when they wake up. Despite our best efforts to plan and control our lives, the reality is that we can't predict the future with much certainty. Dealing with people, technology, weather, and countless other variables guarantees that life remains unpredictable.

The problem with this? Uncertainty is uncomfortable. It's unsettling. It's stressful. Throughout history, humans have sought to understand and predict the world around them to feel in control and safe. Predictability brings comfort while unpredictability brings anxiety—simply because it feels out of our control.

Let's take first dates as an example. Meeting the cutie from your weekly yoga class at your favorite coffee shop probably feels more comfortable than going on a blind date with a stranger at a random café you've never been to. The first scenario feels familiar and fairly predictable, while the second is overflowing with uncertainty. Our brains evolved to be risk averse, prioritizing safety and familiarity over uncertainty. This instinct served our ancestors well (i.e., they didn't go off eating random, potentially poisonous berries), but it can hold back your personal growth today by leading you to avoid new and uncertain experiences.

The fear of the unknown stems from a desire to control what happens next. But life's inherent messiness means we can't control everything. It's impossible. The good news is while you can't always control the events in your life, you *can* always control your reactions to those events. Embracing uncertainty frees you from the pressure of needing to know what happens next and shifts your focus onto how you respond. This mindset fosters resilience and flexibility, and that boosts your confidence in any situation.

View uncertainty as an opportunity to learn more about yourself, to form unexpected social connections, and to grow as a person. Let it show you how you respond to the unexpected, transforming fear into curiosity and anxiety into empowerment. With this mindset, uncertainty suddenly starts to make you feel more creative, innovative, and bold rather than paralyzing you with self-doubt. Under the right circumstances and with the right headspace, unfamiliar situations spark our minds to become more alert and adaptable. They make us feel more empowered and alive.

Over time, repeatedly stepping into uncertainty builds confidence by making discomfort more manageable. It makes uncertainty feel less crippling in your mind and it makes your confidence less contingent upon knowing what to expect. This occurrence, akin to "exposure therapy" in clinical psychology, shows us that the idea of something is often scarier than the actual thing itself. By exposing yourself to uncertain situations, you build emotional resilience and calm your anxiety over time.

Improv theater is an excellent illustration of confidence in the face of uncertainty. When improvisers step onstage, they have no script or predetermined course of action. They must rely on their instincts, responding to their scene partners moment by moment. True improv requires each actor to have great confidence because it demands they find comfort in uncertainty. Seasoned improvisers thrive in unpredictable environments, displaying remarkably high levels of confidence even when they have zero clue what's about to happen in two seconds time.

To become comfortable with uncertainty, practice putting yourself in situations where you don't have all the answers. Embrace the unknown. Remain curious about the uncertain. And stop feeling like you always have to have your next steps planned out. Bathe in the present moment.

This approach will help you build authentic, lasting confidence, allowing you to navigate life's unpredictability with grace and resilience. It encourages you to trust your instincts.

Lesson 2: Trust Your Instincts

Most people overthink way too much. And unfortunately, it doesn't do them much good. Overthinking is a common barrier to confidence, as it stems from self-doubt and a lack of trust in your instincts. Constantly questioning yourself leads to stress, anxiety, and an obsession with hypothetical scenarios that rarely materialize. Ironically, while overthinking can make you feel more assured of yourself in the moment, it does just the opposite in the long run. That's because it invalidates your mind's natural responses and instincts, which are the most authentic expressions of who you really are.

Overthinking stems from self-doubt and a lack of trust in your instincts.

Your brain is a powerful computing machine, capable of generating appropriate responses to almost any situation quickly and efficiently. For instance, when you watch a funny movie and laugh at a silly line, your brain has instinctively responded to humor. Congrats! That's the appropriate response—and it's an *instinct*. Overthinking the decision to laugh would be absurd. Similarly, walking down a busy street involves countless automatic decisions, from stepping aside for a runner passing by to stopping at a traffic light so you don't get hit by a car. If you consciously deliberated each action, thinking it through thoroughly, walking more than a block would be exhausting and chaotic.

Improv thrives on instincts, teaching people to trust their first thoughts and reactions. Trusting your instincts is essential for confidence because it validates your authentic inner voice as credible and worthwhile. Your instincts are the purest form of "you." Respect them how you'd like to respect yourself.

I've seen tons of new improv students fall into the trap of overthinking, believing they need to be funny and clever. They believe they need to think of interesting bits, plan punch lines, and say what they think the audience wants to hear. This approach is awful. It makes these new improvisers stressed out and insecure onstage, as they second-guess their every move.

The more an improviser thinks, the less authentic their performance becomes. And the less authentic their performance appears, the less entertaining or believable it seems. Confidence works the same way.

Let's be real—thinking all the time is exhausting. Surrendering the need to overthink frees improvisers from the cognitive pain of plotting and planning. It frees them of self-consciousness and pushes them into the flow of the present moment. Trusting their instincts allows them to act spontaneously and speak naturally, making their performances more engaging, fluid, and relatable.

Audiences connect with improvisers who act from their instincts because these reactions feel candid and authentic. They come across as *real people doing real things.* The more an improviser goes with their instincts, the less they doubt themselves, the more authentic they appear, and the more confident they feel. The same happens in real everyday life, with real everyday people.

Overthinking paralyzes your mind with self-doubt, preventing you from trusting your authentic inner voice. In most situations, within reason, your first instinct is the most genuine and accurate response. It's what you should do. Trusting your instincts enables you to stay true to yourself, relying on your internal compass and judgment. By learning to trust your instincts, you develop a deeper sense of self-assurance and confidence from a place of authenticity and self-respect.

Lesson 3: Embrace Failure

One reason why it's hard to trust your instincts in moments of uncertainty is the fear of failure. From a young age, many people learn to see failure as unequivocally bad, especially in school. Poor grades signal academic failure, running slowly in gym class signals athletic failure, and difficulty making friends signals social failure. When shunned as a bad thing, failure feels devastating, instilling in young people a sense of weakness, shame, and incapability. Sadly, these feelings can linger for a lifetime.

When people enter adulthood, they often take this mindset with them, living with a deep-seated fear of failure that deters them from trying new things. This fear fosters a fixed mindset where failure is seen as a reflection of one's inherent inadequacy. When you fear failure, you reinforce self-doubt, take negative outcomes personally, and hesitate to act. In short, you paralyze your initiative and stunt your confidence.

Viewing failure as a weakness makes it difficult to believe in yourself. The fear of failure prevents you from setting new goals, let alone ever achieving them. This fear can become a self-fulfilling prophecy as focusing on possible failures makes you feel mentally stuck. It can make you self-sabotage, whether intentionally or not, ultimately bringing about the very failure you feared. Each failure reinforces your belief in your inadequacy, creating a vicious cycle that's hard to escape.

True confidence requires a mindset that celebrates failure. Accept failure as a normal, healthy part of life and view each failure as a new opportunity to learn and grow. This mindset allows you to maintain your confidence during times you do fail, recognizing that failure not as a signal of weakness but as a chance to build resilience.

Failure isn't a sign of weakness; it's a chance to build resilience.

Improv celebrates failure. Because actors navigate improv scenes unprepared, making everything up as they go, they're bound to make mistakes. These blunders are often gifts in disguise as they create the most memorable and entertaining moments of a scene. They help improvisers figure out what the scene could look like, opening their eyes to ideas they would never have thought to plan. When an improviser makes a mistake, they roll with it. They choose to make fun of it, even making the mistake over and over again for comedic effect. They milk it for laughs, stripping away its negative value and making it positive. They might even learn something from it. Mistakes are inevitable, and they're only bad if you view them as bad.

While life doesn't always allow you to turn mistakes into entertainment, you can always choose how you respond to the mistakes you make. Consider the story of Thomas Edison, famed innovator who invented the light bulb. While working on the very first light bulb, Edison failed thousands of times. Yet he learned something new from each failure, and so he tried something new. He embraced failure and saw it as a natural part of his journey that offered him a chance to grow. Edison famously said, "I have not failed. I've just found 10,000 ways that won't work."

An overwhelming fear of failure can feel paralyzing, but embracing failure transforms mistakes into opportunities for growth. The more you embrace failure, the more comfortable you become with taking risks. The more times you take risks and chase your goals, the less weight any concerns about failure have over your mind.

Let each time you fail at something remind you that you had the confidence to put yourself out there, take a risk, and go for it. Let it validate your ability to show confidence.

Embracing failure doesn't mean denying your limitations or ignoring risk. It means seeing failure for what it is—not for the self-doubts and anxieties it may trigger. When you fail at something, it's a sign you're discovering your capabilities while expanding them to new heights.

The way I see it, failure is a hidden precursor to growth. Treating failure as a positive experience gives you the mental and emotional strength to recover from disappointments and maintain belief in your abilities. When you see failure as beneficial, you cultivate a growth mindset, recognizing that failure simply marks progress you've yet to achieve.

Embracing failure builds humility, authenticity, and healthy vulnerability, laying the foundation for true confidence. Admitting mistakes and learning from them shows self-awareness and willingness to grow, making you stronger as a result. In the words of tennis legend Roger Federer, "Even top-ranked tennis players win barely more than half of the points they play . . . the best in the world are not the best because they win every point; it's because they know they'll lose again and again and have learned how to deal with it."

Lesson 4: Drop Your Agenda

When people fear uncertainty, second-guess their instincts, and worry about failure, they often cope by developing an agenda—a set of fixed expectations for how they believe a situation should unfold. For instance, if you're stepping into a work meeting, you might be adamant about pushing a specific proposal, regardless of how the group discussion evolves. This can give you a temporary sense of control. However, having an agenda can lower your adaptability and stifle your confidence over time, as that makes it difficult to respond effectively to the present moment. While your coworkers are already discussing the next proposal, you're still stuck thinking of ways to sell them on the one they shot down ten minutes ago.

Although an agenda may provide a temporary sense of confidence, it's an inherently inflexible way of thinking. Clinging to an agenda suppresses the natural flow of any situation you step into, making it impossible for you to adapt and respond authentically. Agendas are easily threatened when things don't go as planned, setting up your anxiety to rise and your confidence to fall.

Improv teaches the importance of dropping your agenda. Improvisers won't succeed if they cling to preconceived ideas and expectations about how the scene might go; they succeed by dynamically responding to the scene as it unfolds. Beginners in improv often struggle with letting go of their agenda because they fear uncertainty and don't trust their instincts. What they haven't realized yet is that the only thing stopping them from being fully present is themselves.

In life, adhering strictly to an agenda limits your psychological flexibility and undermines your confidence in unpredictable situations. Dropping your agenda is crucial for developing lasting confidence. Instead of planning every move, focus on the present moment and respond to what's actually happening right here, right now. Agendas are fantasies. And fantasies aren't real.

Letting go of your agenda builds up your confidence by enabling you to respond effectively to the present moment. When you're not fixated on a predetermined plan, you become more attuned to the people around you. You listen more to what they're saying and you gain a better sense of how they feel. This allows you to make better decisions based on real-time feedback from others, adapting to the flow of conversations and events. Without an agenda, you're more open to unexpected opportunities and can evaluate new information with a clear mind. Everyone benefits as a result, including yourself and those around you.

In improv, there's a mindset of "yes, and." It means accepting whatever your scene partner offers and building upon it. I think of real life as one big improv scene, and the people around you are your scene partners. The "yes, and" mindset encourages you to accept your current situation and validate others' perspectives rather than questioning or denying their legitimacy. It allows you to respond appropriately to the present moment rather than acting from a preconceived agenda you had a few minutes ago.

Adopting a "yes, and" mindset in life can make you a better communicator, reduce your stress levels, and increase your confidence. Embracing unexpected opportunities—rather than resisting them—allows you to find new and innovative ways to express yourself and achieve your goals. This mindset reinforces the belief that while you can't always control what happens in life, you can always control how you respond.

By dropping your agenda and embracing the present, you cultivate a powerfully confident mindset, equipping you to navigate whatever life throws your way.

All it takes is a little improvisation.

CONFIDENCE, DISTILLED

Stop Overplanning. Rigid planning can undermine your confidence by preventing you from adapting to the unexpected.

Embrace Uncertainty. Accept that life is unpredictable and choose to navigate its uncertainties with openness and curiosity.

Trust Your Instincts. Stop overthinking or second-guessing yourself. Let your instincts guide you.

Embrace Failure. View mistakes as opportunities for learning and growth rather than as reflections of your worth.

Adopt a "Yes, and" Mindset. Let go of rigid agendas. Focus on the present moment, accept it as it is, and respond to it with openness and creativity.

KEY #2
ADAPTIVE RESILIENCE

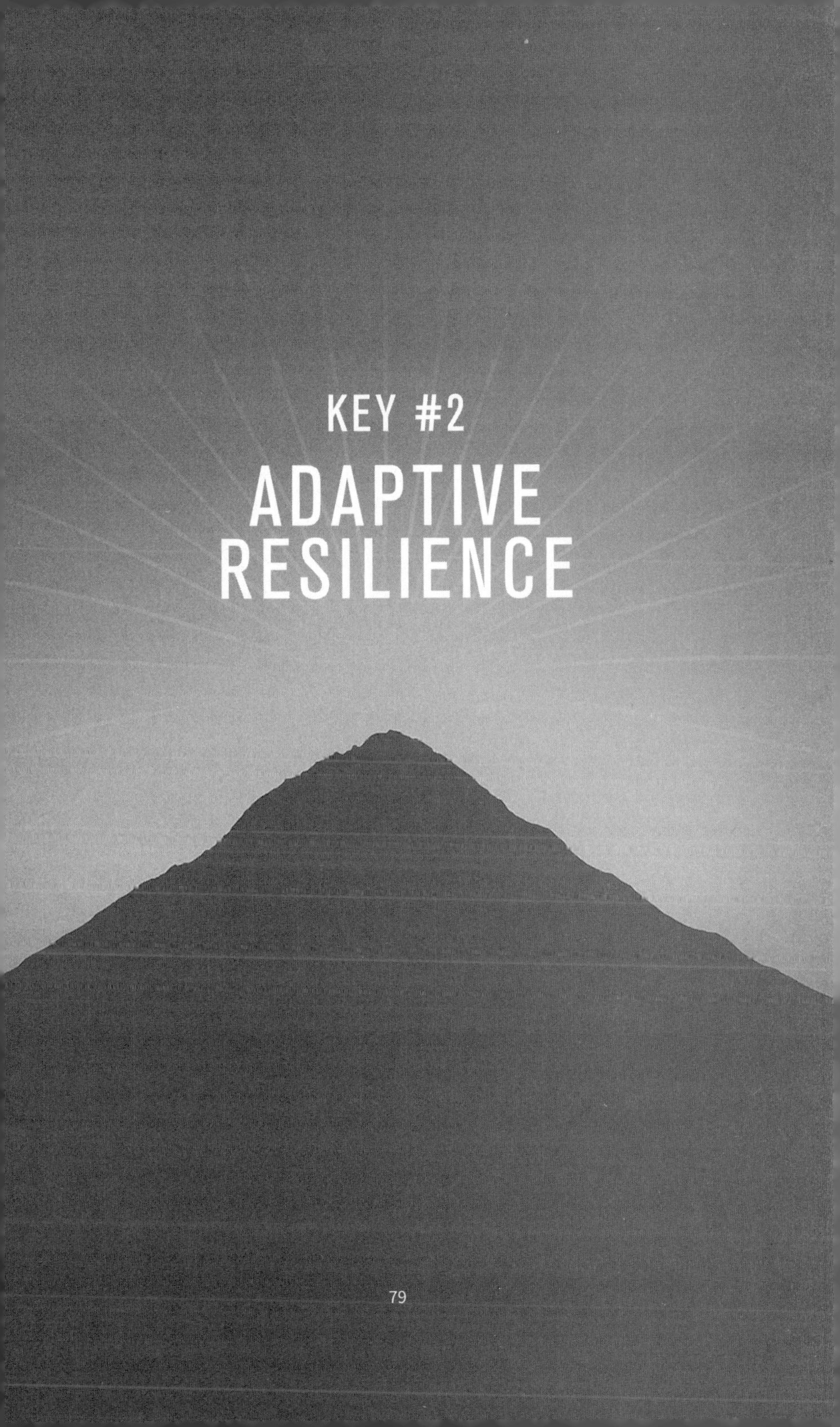

Chapter 5

RESILIENCE IN THE FACE OF DOUBT

When I was five years old, my physiatrist wrote me an odd prescription: Enroll in a karate class. Apparently, hours on hours of physical therapy and occupational therapy weren't enough treatment for my body. It was time to think outside the box and start chopping some blocks.

While I didn't see it at the time, my doc was onto something. Karate has all the ingredients of an ideal physical therapy program for a kid with cerebral palsy. Karate involves body movements that improve coordination, combating the naturally awkward movements that come with the condition. It increases flexibility, loosening up stiff muscles and tight joints. And it improves balance and core stability, which could help children with cerebral palsy—like young me—walk more steadily, stumble less, and move with more agility.

I was naturally excited to take up karate—not for these benefits, but because I wanted to be like the superheroes I saw in movies and the wrestlers I watched on TV. I wasn't thinking about my coordination, flexibility, or balance. I just wanted to punch and kick stuff. I was a five-year-old kid, after all, and I wanted to fit in with all the other kids I knew who could play sports and move around freely. I wanted to feel *able.* Little did I know, the first time I set foot in a karate studio was almost my last.

I loved my first karate class. But after it ended, the instructor pulled my mom aside for a brief chat. When he insisted that she reconsider my enrollment in his program, my mom was shocked. She assured him that while I might not be able to do everything the same way as the other kids in his class, I'd adapt and find my own way. She told him she realized my hands might not fully open for a crisp chop or close all the way for a perfect punch, but that wasn't what mattered; I was there to challenge myself and grow. Still, the instructor remained skeptical, only begrudgingly letting me stay in his class. His concern, I later realized, wasn't just about whether my body could keep up; it was whether he thought my mind could.

People have all kinds of biases and stereotypes when they meet someone different from them, and encountering someone with a disability is no exception. Too often, assumptions rush in before understanding has a chance. People with disabilities often grow up feeling stigmatized, devalued, and socially excluded. I know firsthand what it's like to be counted out at first glance.

When other people doubt your abilities, it's easy to start doubting yourself. It's easy to rethink your worth and to believe your goals might not be worth pursuing—to believe that those goals aren't meant for people like you.

I was fortunate to have parents who rejected toxic stereotypes and instead told me I could do anything I set my mind to. I might not do it the same way as my peers, they said, but I could figure out my own way and celebrate my effort. My parents insisted I stay in that karate class, and it instantly became one of my favorite hobbies.

If you're not careful, other people's doubts can quietly become your own.

Six years later, that same instructor who doubted me awarded me a brown belt.

WHEN OTHERS' DOUBTS BECOME YOUR OWN

Early in my life, I learned that although some people would see me for what they believed I could not do, I had to see myself for how I could do things differently. I could become the person I wanted to be, defying other people's expectations along the way.

I get a certain thrill in proving others wrong. But it's not about showing them they were wrong. It's about proving to myself I'm the only one with the power to say what I can and can't do. When someone doubts me, I get an opportunity to focus on my own resilience and drive. I turn their doubt into my motivation.

To turn doubt into motivation, you have to disentangle the process by which other people's doubts about you become your own doubts about yourself. This disentanglement starts with seeing someone else's uncertainty for what it actually is: a projection of their own insecurity. Most of the time, when someone doubts your abilities, they're revealing more about themselves than exposing you. They're engaging in an ugly psychological defense mechanism called "projection."

Projection happens when a person doubts someone else because they're uncomfortable with their own insecurities. They project their own self-doubts onto the other person. When someone projects, they avoid confronting their own insecurities. They shift their focus away from their internal struggles and onto the other person, which lets them feel a temporary sense of relief from the weight of their own issues. For instance, if someone doubts their own competence, they might doubt others' competence to even the playing field, making themselves feel more adequate by putting others down.

Take relationships as an example. Someone with a history of failed relationships might doubt other people's abilities to maintain healthy relationships because they're projecting their own insecurities outward. They might make comments like "Are you sure you're ready for this commitment?" simply because they themselves feel unready for commitment or have experienced traumatic disappointments in the past.

Or consider career choice. A parent might doubt their child's decision to pursue a less-conventional career path—say, becoming an artist or entrepreneur—because they themselves fear the uncertainty and risk attached to that kind of lifestyle. The parent's own preference for stability and their anxiety with uncertainty can make them project their own doubt onto their child simply to get a sense of validation and relief from their own insecurity.

Many self-doubts people develop in their lives originate from other people's projections, but those projections simply represent someone else's misplaced inner turmoil. The wild thing about projection is people often do it without any conscious awareness or malintent. They don't project their own issues onto you on purpose or with any desire to bring you down. Projection just happens. It's as natural to the brain as is the instinct to breathe or blink.

In my own life, I've been doubted in sports, school, dating—and even in writing this very book. More than a few people said it would never be published. Yet here you are, reading it.

Far too often, people let others' doubts about them hold them back, which is unfortunate because those doubts are usually a load of unfounded nonsense. When someone doubts you, it typically says more about their own insecurities than about your true potential. You shouldn't take it personally.

When someone doubts you, it typically says more about their own insecurities than about your true potential.

AUTHORING YOUR OWN LIFE STORY

To stop other people's projections from damaging your self-confidence, you need to recognize that their insecurities are *theirs* to deal with—not yours. This is particularly important for introverts to hear loud and clear, as their reflective nature can make them more likely to internalize external doubts more deeply. Any time someone doubts you, take a moment to question whether their doubt is valid or offers you any useful new information.

To sort the helpful from the harmful, ask yourself:

- Does this person have relevant experience or knowledge about what I'm trying to do?
- Is their feedback about the action I'm taking, or is it about me as a person?
- Does it feel like their feedback is coming from a place of care and concern, or from fear, insecurity, and limitation?

- Do they genuinely want me to succeed, or might my success threaten them in some way?
- Does their feedback align with my own values and goals?

If your answers point to genuine, trustworthy, and compassionate insight, it's probably worth reflecting on. But if it feels rooted in their fear, insecurity, or ignorance, it's projection—not guidance.

Before taking someone's doubts to heart, run through this list of questions. A lot of the time, you'll find that their doubts are nonsense and have everything to do with them and not you. At the end of the day, doubt is just subjective feedback, not fact. Remember, you're the author of your life story. The pen's in your hands, not theirs.

Doubt is feedback, not fact.

People often forget that they're their own author, possessing the power to pen their own journey—and at a great loss. Those who view their life story as prewritten by others tend to lack confidence because they fall into the toxic victim mentality where they soak up others' doubts and internalize them as their own. These people see themselves as passive protagonists in their lives without any agency or ability to become their own guide. When other people doubt them, they accept this doubt as valid. As a result, their self-doubt grows and erodes their confidence, like a heavy weight dragging them down until they eventually fatigue and stagnate.

Feeling like your abilities are called into question can be incredibly disheartening, making you lose faith in yourself. But when you see yourself as the author of your own life story, you can stop other people's doubts about you from turning into your own doubts about yourself. This self-authorship mindset is a hallmark of adaptive resilience. It's crucial for developing confidence because it gives you a sense of agency and control that your mind needs to flourish.

A key part of becoming the author of your own story is letting go of the need for external validation. Conforming to social standards that earn others' approval is a natural instinct, rooted in our deep desire as social creatures to fit in and belong. Most people want to be liked, and being applauded, admired, and congratulated feels good. However, when the instinct for social approval influences too much of your decision-making, you lose the ability to act authentically, and you place your confidence in the hands of others. This external focus makes your confidence shaky, as it only emerges when you receive a certain level of external validation. In essence, it's social dependency.

The more weight you place on external social approval, the more damaging it is when people doubt you; they're two sides of the same coin. Authentic confidence can come only from within. It's based on how you feel about yourself regardless of what others think. When you rely on external validation, your confidence becomes fragile and out of your control. That's a dangerous game to play.

You can't always choose what abilities you have, but you can always choose how you apply them. When you let other people write your life story, you deny yourself that choice. When you derive your confidence from the approval of others and let it fade because they doubt you, you forget that choice even exists. I say it's time to put that choice into your own hands.

TURNING DOUBT INTO MOTIVATION

By the time I was ten years old, I'd worked my way up to a third-level brown belt in karate. I learned how other people's doubts could fuel my own motivation, a lesson I applied when I doubled down on my desire to tell my own tale. Sometimes, it takes someone doubting you to ignite that desire for self-determination and drive you to pursue a goal to the fullest. Recognizing and nurturing this internal source of strength can be incredibly empowering.

For decades, psychologists have studied self-determination theory, which says people need to feel in control of their life in order to thrive psychologically. When you feel like someone else is determining your fate, it weighs you down mentally and makes it hard to muster the energy, effort, or passion to perform well at a task. But when you feel like you're determining your own fate, you feel energized and empowered.

A few years ago, I founded a company called The Match Lab. It's a dating coaching service where I help people improve their online dating profiles. When I first started developing the company, a few people in my life were wary. They thought it'd fail and cautioned me against pursuing it. While I was disappointed by this discouragement, I tried to see their skepticism for what it truly was: either subconscious projections or well-intended guidance. I knew the harsh reality that most new businesses fail. Starting a business is tough, so it makes sense that most people feel anxious about the idea of starting their own business and might project that anxiety outward onto a new entrepreneur. I also knew these people in my life cared about me and would have only my best interests at heart. Their advice walked a fine line between projection and guidance.

Because I'd had past experiences when people doubted what I could accomplish, I was used to questioning others' misgivings rather than immediately internalizing them. By this stage in my life, hearing their doubts actually reaffirmed my commitment to pursuing my new company because I'd learned that when people doubt you, it usually means you're setting out to do something ambitious.

Ambition isn't just a motivational spark; it's confidence in motion—proof you believe in your abilities to achieve your goals. Ambition is believing you're capable of more tomorrow than you are today. When I started The Match Lab, I viewed others' doubts as evidence that I had the self-belief to do something ambitious, and in that way, their doubts validated and further fueled my confidence in myself. I was already in motion.

When someone tells me I can do something, I know I can do it. When someone tells me I *can't* do something, I know I'll do it twice as well.

> **When someone tells me I can do something, I know I can do it. When someone tells me I *can't* do something, I know I'll do it twice as well.**

Whether with karate or The Match Lab, my experiences being doubted didn't lead me to resent those who questioned me; rather, I felt compassion toward them because I realized they may be struggling with their own insecurities. Their doubt didn't lead me to give up; it validated my identity as an ambitious person. It fueled my drive to be the author of my own story. And being doubted didn't make me preoccupied with proving those who doubted me wrong. Instead, I wanted to prove myself right—to develop my resilience and to remind myself that I'm the only one with the power to say what I can and can't do.

When you can see other people's doubts for the projections they really are, you can prevent them from becoming doubts you have about yourself. You won't just prevent their doubts from limiting your confidence; you can use them as a hidden source of confidence you've yet to channel.

Listen to your gut and pursue the goals that matter to you, even when those in positions of authority or those you trust count you out. Feel at ease in deciding not to take others' doubts personally and take pride in knowing that only you can know your own worth. Remember that you always have the final say in what you make of your abilities.

YOU HAVE NOTHING TO PROVE TO ANYONE BUT YOURSELF

After getting my brown belt in karate, I joined my middle school's wrestling team, where I was not just the smallest guy on the team but also the only disabled kid. After wrestling, I joined the swim team and, after that, the tennis team. While my coaches welcomed me to each team, they made it clear they wouldn't let me off easy or give me any special treatment because of my disability. I'd have to do every drill and exercise everyone else on the team did, and if I wanted special treatment, I knew where the door was. They believed I deserved a spot on the team, and it was up to me to show myself I believed that, too.

When you get used to people doubting you, encountering those who believe in you can be an unfamiliar feeling. Savor those encounters. Let them remind you that you have nothing to prove to anyone but yourself. And the best thing to prove to yourself is your resilience.

Resilience is an inner gold mine that gives you confidence in any situation. More than your talent, ambition, or achievement, resilience keeps you going when you face any kind of challenge—whether it's having someone doubt your ability, experiencing a setback while pursuing a goal, or feeling dejected and like you might not be able to succeed as you thought you could initially.

I often think of resilience as a mental strength that comes from having overcome adversity in the past. But resilience doesn't just come from prevailing over past challenges. It comes from rethinking present challenges as opportunities for growth and self-care.

Resilience doesn't just come from overcoming your past—it's turning present challenges into opportunities for growth.

Resilience means embracing failure and showing compassion for your struggles. It's believing that your abilities aren't innate but can be developed through effort, perseverance, and learning from your experiences. It's viewing failures as temporary setbacks and valuable opportunities to learn something new rather than as signals of your abilities. When you affirm your resilience, you define yourself by your effort, not by your outcome.

Resilience is the difference between remaining confident versus crumbling when life gets tough. When you feel your confidence dwindle in the face of any challenge, take a moment to remember how far you've come throughout life and how much you've accomplished in other challenging pursuits. Understand that no meaningful success comes without failure, adversity, and moments of weakness along the way. Acknowledge the progress you've made now and at other times when you've grown through your efforts, developing skills you didn't have before. Taking pride in the journey builds adaptive resilience that can translate into lasting confidence. That's a gift of confidence only you can give yourself.

DOUBTS ARE OPPORTUNITIES FOR RESILIENCE

When I was a toddler, medical professionals doubted I would ever be able to walk properly without assistance. They doubted I'd be able to learn in conventional schools alongside able-bodied students or lead an independent life as an adult. Their doubts were neither personal nor projective; they were based on a scientific understanding of cerebral palsy. But letting other people's expectations dictate my future—no matter how credible those expectations were—would have meant committing myself to a life of limitations and unfulfilled potential. It feels disconcerting to reflect on these early prognoses and imagine an alternative life where I didn't pursue my goals while believing in my ability. Other people's perceptions can shape our own reality if we let them.

I've come to understand others' doubts as opportunities to redefine my own limits. When others express doubt about your abilities, it's natural to feel hurt, angry, or discouraged. But when you see their doubt as a product of their own personal experiences and an exposure of their subconscious insecurities, you realize it's not an accurate assessment of your potential.

Even when doubt stings, it offers you an opportunity to build confidence through resilience and self-affirmation, challenging you to double down on your belief in your abilities. Each new doubt you question lets you see the world and yourself more clearly and compassionately. It adds to your resilience, priming your mind to find confidence in the next doubt you encounter.

CONFIDENCE, DISTILLED

Recognize Doubt as Projection. When other people doubt you, it usually says more about their own insecurities than your abilities or potential.

Author Your Own Story. Only you can define what you're capable of.

Use Doubt as Motivation. Channel others' doubts into motivation, viewing them as opportunities to push your limits and demonstrate your resilience.

Do It for Yourself. Know that you have nothing to prove to anyone but yourself.

Chapter 6

STAYING COOL UNDER PRESSURE

My former table tennis teammate Daryl is a juggernaut of an athlete. I've known Daryl for over a decade, and he's a formidable competitor. Standing over six feet tall, with herculean muscles and a pterodactyl wingspan, Daryl's stature alone is enough to strip away your confidence before he even serves you the ball. Add on his impeccable form, quick reflexes, and tactical table tennis IQ, and it's no wonder why Daryl is a repeat medalist at top international tournaments.

Many years ago, Daryl and I were on the U.S. National Team together. Whenever we played practice matches, he'd wipe the floor with me. I looked up to Daryl and wanted to be like him on the table: calm, powerful, and unshakable. Dominant. A true winner.

On Sunday, December 17, 2023, Daryl was the only obstacle standing between me and a U.S. Open gold medal.

After nearly a decade as teammates, we'd collided on this day as competitors on a grand stage for the first time. Frankly, it felt like a miracle that I'd even made it to the finals. Facing Daryl, now, sent shivers down my spine.

I knew I'd never beaten Daryl in the past, and while I was playing the best table tennis of my life that tournament, it was hard to see why this day would be any different. Waiting for our match to start, my anxiety started rising and my confidence dwindled as I began counting myself out, doubting my ability to compete with Daryl. My mind focused on the outcome I so desperately sought—the coveted gold medal—and the slim chance I had of achieving it. I was beating myself before even giving Daryl the chance to beat me. Enter performance anxiety.

Performance anxiety—also known as stage fright—is one of the most common anxieties people experience, and athletes are no exception. It arises in situations where you feel like you're being evaluated based on your success or failure. It's when you worry so much about succeeding that your worry becomes crippling anxiety, and that anxiety prevents you from being able to succeed at all. Performance anxiety affects everyone, but introverts are particularly susceptible to it due to their heightened sensitivity to external stimuli and their tendencies to self-reflect and overthink. That's why the pressure of being in the spotlight can feel especially intense when you're introverted, often triggering a cascade of anxious thoughts and emotions.

Most people can relate to the feeling of performance anxiety when they've felt nervous in a job interview, taken a standardized test, given a presentation at work, acted onstage, or competed in organized sports. It's the sweaty palms, racing heart, dry mouth, trembling muscles, and flood of negative thoughts.

I know performance anxiety all too well in the table tennis arena, and it's why I've often played like a champion in practice one day and then lost miserably in a tournament the next. When cerebral palsy meets performance anxiety, the results are disastrous. Even in a normal situation when my mind is perfectly calm, every single muscle in my body shakes with tremors. So when my mind fills with anxiety, a tremor storm erupts.

When I stepped up to the table to face Daryl, my hands shook so violently with tremors that I struggled to even hold my paddle. My legs wobbled beneath me with each step, and I found myself missing warm-up shots I'd honed from two decades of practice. As I sensed any remaining inklings of confidence leaving my mind, I knew I needed to calm down and restore my belief in myself. When Daryl and I finished warming up and were preparing to start the match, I stepped a few feet away from the table, sat down on the floor, and closed my eyes. I breathed slow deep breaths, in and out. Honestly, it felt like a weird thing to do. But I ignored the perplexed glances surrounding me and gave myself this one moment I knew I needed. When I felt my heartbeat slow down and my muscles ease up a bit, I stood up and walked to the table to hit my opening serve.

The match would end when either Daryl or I won three games, and after each game finished, I repeated my breathing ritual. I sat, eyes closed, drawing out each inhale and exhale for as long as I could count the seconds going by.

As I played against Daryl, I became the calm, powerful, and unshakable force I was in practice, bringing my highest game to the grand stage. I managed to hold my ground as Daryl and I traded game for game, culminating in a tie-breaking game five.

The fifth game saw Daryl and I trade serve for serve and shot for shot until we arrived at match point—me in the lead by a margin of one. While I felt my muscles tremor as I processed the stakes of the situation, I channeled all of the breathwork I could to feel calm and in control of my mind. I served the ball, and after Daryl returned it back at me, my next shot was the last on that table before a gold medal was draped around my neck.

WHY BEING UNDER PRESSURE KILLS CONFIDENCE

When you feel like you're under any kind of pressure, it can be hard to stay confident. Whether you feel like you're being evaluated by someone else or you've placed the high stakes on yourself, it's natural to experience performance anxiety. The problem is that this anxiety, no matter how natural it is, holds you back from performing to your full potential. Ironically, feeling anxious about performing poorly causes you to perform poorly.

When you fear being judged or failing to meet expectations, that anxiety triggers a stress response in your mind and body. Your brain initiates a complex series of physiological processes throughout your body. Your sympathetic nervous system flares up, making your heart beat faster, your mouth feel drier, and your muscles feel tighter. This phenomenon is commonly known as the fight-or-flight response. It's when adrenaline rushes throughout your body. In small amounts, this increase in nervous system activity helps you perform better. A small dose of adrenaline makes you more focused, alert, and energized. However, in performative settings, nerves and anxiety often cause an excessive response, sending the sympathetic nervous system into overdrive. This heightened state can be especially challenging for introverts, whose nervous systems are more sensitive and reactive to stimulation. Managing this response, though, is crucial for maintaining optimal confidence and performance.

When you're under pressure and experiencing anxiety, your ability to perform well plummets, no matter what kind of task you're trying to perform. As you feel your heart pumping, your body trembling, and your mind racing, your belief in your abilities dwindles and self-consciousness ensues, ultimately eroding your confidence. And when you no longer feel confident, you're even more susceptible to further performance anxiety as the weight of all that pressure suddenly feels insurmountable.

When performance anxiety kicks in, intrusive thoughts and self-doubt usually follow. For example, a student taking an important exam might start questioning their knowledge and abilities as they feel the pressure in the testing room, despite having prepared for this day all month. A basketball player might hear the crowd roaring as she goes for the game-winning free throw, forgetting for a moment how to shoot such a simple and familiar shot as she crumbles under the pressure. Even the most talented, highly trained, experienced superstars in their fields can feel their confidence fly out the window in a high-pressure situation as they suddenly doubt their ability to succeed at the task at hand. This self-doubt can create a vicious cycle where the fear of failing becomes a self-fulfilling prophecy, leading you to actually fail because of that fear.

Performance anxiety is the ultimate confidence killer because it takes a heavy toll on both your mental *and* your physical abilities. Mentally, it obliterates your sense of calm, causing you to engage in negative self-talk where you doubt your abilities and tell yourself that failure is inevitable. Telling yourself—or other people—things like "I can't do this" or "I just know I'm going to mess up" are common side effects of performance anxiety. They're the cognitive distortions that eat away at your confidence.

Physically, performance anxiety leads to a sense of unfamiliarity in your own body. An elite athlete might suddenly find their coordination and reflexes compromised as they feel their muscles tense up and their heart pound out of their chest. A professional musician might find their hands trembling, making them feel like a novice as they try to play the guitar they've practiced for decades. A student walking across stage to receive their diploma at a graduation ceremony might feel like they suddenly forgot how to walk, needing to consciously think "right, left, right, left" just to avoid stumbling in front of the crowd. And the valedictorian at that graduation ceremony? They might trip over their words as they feel the weight of a thousand eyes on them.

INHALE PRESSURE, EXHALE CONFIDENCE

The good news is that you can train your brain to stay confident under pressure. The best way to achieve this is through mindfulness meditation, which builds your resilience against performance anxiety and helps you manage overstimulation.

Mindfulness meditation provides self-grounding and relaxation techniques that allow you to manage your stress levels, reduce the mental and physical symptoms of anxiety, and stay calmly present in high-pressure situations. Meditation is crucial for introverts because it allows them to recharge and build up their tolerance to stimulation, making almost any situation feel less overwhelming.

The easiest, quickest, and most versatile technique within mindfulness meditation is breathwork. This means paying attention to your breathing, slowing it down, and taking a moment to get it under your full control.

Your breath is with you everywhere you go. Each moment of each day and night, you're breathing air in and out. Usually, this breathing occurs subconsciously, without your awareness or control. Neural regions within your brainstem regulate your respiratory system automatically, setting rhythmic breathing patterns that effortlessly transition between inhalation and exhalation.

Because the brainstem operates on an instinctive subconscious level, it's highly sensitive to the fight-or-flight response brought on by anxiety. When you feel anxious, your brainstem goes haywire, sending your mind and body into maximum-alert mode. Your sympathetic nervous system revs up, adrenaline flows through your veins, and your breathing becomes more rapid and shallow as your heart pumps faster. This change in breathing creates the physical sensation of anxiety, and it's common for people to hyperventilate and feel lightheaded soon after. Your muscles tense up and you might even feel like you're suffocating. In extreme cases, this leads to a panic attack. At a lower level of stress, this sensation can linger indefinitely as a chronic sense of anxiety and tightness.

Your breath is the remote control for your nervous system. Use it to change the channel.

Practicing breathwork—where you consciously control your breathing—is an incredibly effective way to manage anxiety and calm your mind. That's because breathwork directly disrupts your body's physical response to stress. It literally changes which part of your brain controls your breathing pattern, taking it out of the grasp of your brainstem (which operates subconsciously and is highly sensitive to stress) and placing it into the hands of your cerebral cortex (which you can control consciously and harness to reduce stress).

This process of breathwork reduces stress and restores confidence by balancing out your autonomic nervous system, forcing your body to relax. You quiet down your body's fight-or-flight stress response and allow your heartbeat to slow back down, your muscles to loosen up, and your mind to regain a sense of calm.

Breathwork is a powerful tool for lowering anxiety and boosting confidence because it's available to you everywhere you go. You always have it at your disposal. Whether you're driving through traffic, lying in bed at night, or about to deliver an important presentation at work, you always have the ability to focus on your breath and control the flow of air in and out of your body.

The simplest breathwork exercise for reducing anxiety is called box breathing. I like to think of it as the four-four-four technique. First, inhale deeply and slowly through your nose for a count of four seconds. As you inhale, count in your head "one, two, three, four" as the seconds go by, drawing out your inhale so it lasts all four seconds. Next, hold your breath for four more seconds, keeping all that air inside you. Finally, exhale slowly for another count of four. You'll feel the most benefit if you repeat this twelve-second inhale-exhale cycle at least a few times. If you can keep repeating it for several minutes, that's even better.

Box breathing is the technique I used when I sat on the floor during my table tennis match at the U.S. Open. It's what brought me down from a state of panic to a sense of calm. Box breathing helps balance out your nervous system, lowers stress, and improves mental focus. It's easy, quick, and feels good, too. It's an incredibly beneficial technique for introverts, who can use it to manage overwhelming sensations that arise from overstimulation and anxiety in social or performance-based situations.

Another effective breathwork exercise is deep diaphragmatic breathing. First, sit or lie down in a comfortable position. Place one hand on your chest and the other on your abdomen. Next, inhale deeply through your nose for four seconds, allowing your abdomen to rise while keeping your chest relatively still. Then, exhale slowly through your mouth for another four seconds, allowing your abdomen to fall. Repeat this inhale and exhale for a few minutes, focusing your attention on the rise and fall of your abdomen. This exercise promotes a full exchange of oxygen, slows down your heartbeat, and stabilizes your blood pressure.

Controlling your breath is such a simple practice, and it's easy to overlook the power of breathwork. Focusing on your breath pulls your mind and body out of panic mode, putting you back in the driver's seat of your thoughts. It anchors your mind in the present moment, effortlessly pulling your attention away from anxious thoughts and creating a meditative state of mental clarity and emotional stability. In doing so, breathwork counteracts self-doubts and makes it easier to feel confident. For introverts, it's an essential tool for thriving in an extroverted world.

Control your breath, control your confidence.

MEDITATING YOUR WAY TO CONFIDENCE

I first started dabbling in meditation when I was a senior in college. I went to Cornell University in rural upstate New York, which was the perfect place to find moments of calm in the outdoors. Surrounded by mountains, lakes, and waterfalls, I would bathe in the present moment, letting the sounds of nature fill my mind. I'd silence my phone, find a quiet place to sit, and just breathe as a scenic view consumed my attention.

Later in my twenties, once I'd moved to Los Angeles, I tried my first meditation retreat. I did a weekend of solitude in silence, where I neither spoke with anyone nor used any technology. Each moment from when I woke in the morning until I slept at night, I was meditating. For most of the time, I sat or lay down. Other times, I went out for walks. And of course, I also ate and bathed. The aim was to observe my mind in its purest form, without the noise of my own voice; without any engagement with other people; and without any form of technology, media, or entertainment. Zero distractions from my internal sense of self.

Since then, I've continued to do a five-day silent meditation retreat each year. These retreats have taught me a lot about how the mind works and have helped me recognize the hidden roadblocks to confidence. The biggest insight I've gained from my time in deep meditation is that the most significant barrier to your own confidence isn't your skill set, life experiences, or goals; it's your ego.

The biggest barrier to confidence isn't your skill set, life experiences, or goals. It's your ego.

The Curse of Ego

When I say "ego" here, I don't mean arrogance or the egotistical sense of the word. I mean the mental construct of "I" and "me," the sense of self your mind creates and clings to. It's the feeling of self-identity that links your past to your present and your present to your future, like a story arc your mind is constantly writing.

Your ego is the loudest part of your mind, and it dictates most of your daily awareness. It's the conscious voice in your head that you identify with in order to feel a tangible sense of "me." Your ego regulates your desires and impulses, allows you to plan ahead for the future, gives you the ability to think logically, and makes you feel ecstatic when you succeed at something. But your ego is also responsible for your ability to feel self-conscious, insecure, jealous, narcissistic, and dejected. It's easily hurt by criticism or failure. It's the part of your mind that makes high-stakes situations feel like immense psychological pressure.

Your ego is both a blessing and a curse, providing you with both pleasant and unpleasant experiences as it interprets your reality, makes sense of the world around you, and gives you a sense of identity. The issue with ego, however, is that it's never satisfied. When you experience something pleasant, your ego craves more of it. When you experience something unpleasant, your ego floods your mind with self-destructive thoughts.

Your ego preoccupies your mind with self-image, constant judgment, and fear of deficiency, creating a pervasive barrier to developing and maintaining confidence. For the ego, confidence is superficial and dynamic, fueled by positive external events, and easily eroded by negative ones. That's because your ego attaches your self-worth to an ideal, unsustainable version of yourself and to external achievements that come and go. It always craves *more.*

Constant judgment is another plague of the ego. It encourages your mind to compare yourself with others and judge how you measure up in relation to them. This kind of social comparison creates a precarious sense of self, yielding a lingering sense of inadequacy most often and a false sense of confidence at best.

Lastly, the ego is in constant fear of deficiency. That's part of the reason why it's so easy to slip into that fight-or-flight response, where you sweat, your heart races, and your muscles tremble. Your ego is always on guard, seeking to protect itself from anything that could threaten your self-image. This sets you up to develop fears of vulnerability and failure. The ego doesn't truly cherish positive events; it just ruminates over potential negative events. This chronic fear of deficiency lowers self-esteem, prevents risk-taking, and makes it harder to be resilient, all of which are essential for building confidence.

Do you see what the ego does at its core? It creates self-doubt. It takes you out of the present moment, distorts how you interpret your experiences in life, and prevents you from deriving a sense of confidence from your inner qualities. It fuels anxiety and gets in the way of you ever feeling calm for an extended period of time.

The problem with ego is that it never lives in the present moment. It's always pushing your mind to focus on either the past or the future. The ego is like a novelist, and it wants to write a narrative about your life. But it doesn't want to write a self-serving narrative; all it knows is drama. So, it writes a tumultuous tale, a story that could become a bestseller. That's why we get so sucked into our own ego and let it consume our thoughts. We're engrossed in our own story, for it's imbued with intense emotions, conflicts, and what-ifs. It's defined by triumphs and failures, heroes and victims, traumas and unmet desires—for a novel written about a calm protagonist living a life of contentment would never sell by the millions.

The narrative your ego creates keeps you trapped in cycles of regret, longing, and anxiety as you endlessly replay past mistakes and worry about future uncertainties. The ego thrives on this constant mental noise, creating an illusion of importance and urgency that distracts you from the peace and clarity right in front of you in the present moment. By pulling your attention away from the present moment, the ego prevents you from ever experiencing true contentment or confidence. Instead, you become a passive protagonist in a drama of your own mind's making, endlessly seeking validation and approval through achievement. The ego glorifies an idyllic future you, but this future you will one day become another present you, simply seeking a newly defined idyllic future version of yourself. And the cycle continues . . .

Quieting Your Ego

Mindfulness meditation is a cure that quiets down your ego, allowing you to feel a more effortless and reliable sense of confidence. When you meditate, you shift your mind's attention away from your ego and toward the present moment, observing your thoughts and feelings without emotional attachment or critical judgment. You practice a state of mind called *nonjudgmental awareness.*

Most of us have a strong instinct to label our thoughts as either good or bad. The practice of nonjudgmental awareness challenges this instinct. It involves simply observing and accepting your thoughts as they come and go, without giving them deliberate attention. It's like watching a car drive by on a nearby road. The car comes, exists in front of you for a moment, and then passes out of view. You don't judge what kind of model or make the car is or what color it is. You just observe it. You can train your mind to do the same with your thoughts.

Most of the thoughts and feelings you experience come from your ego, reflecting memories of your past and imaginations of your future. Often, memories of the past yield negative feelings of regret, shame, and loss. Meanwhile, imaginations of the future frequently bring anxiety, fear, and unrealistic expectations. Your ego thrives on these thoughts, because without them, your ego doesn't exist. Your ego *wants* to exist, so it makes you identify with these thoughts, feeling as though they're the truest version of "you." This identification creates in your mind a self-defeating image of yourself based on external past events and a feeling of heightened anxiety as you step into the future.

Meditation helps you recognize thoughts and feelings as products of your ego, allowing you to observe them as passing phenomena rather than internalizing them or assigning them value. In doing so, you can detach from your thoughts and develop a calmer existence. You can view self-destructive thoughts as pointless blabbering from your ego rather than as meaningful insights to read into.

Self-destructive thoughts aren't meaningful insights to read into—they're pointless blabbering from your ego.

Meditation dissolves the constant chatter of the ego, replacing the chronic noise in your mind with a space of inner stillness and clarity. You make room to experience the present moment as it is, without interpreting it as part of your personal narrative. When your mind no longer jumps to construct a narrative, it allows you to experience the present moment with full consciousness, for your attention is no longer consumed by worries about your past or future. You free yourself from your ego's story arc.

As you cultivate this awareness in the here and now, you begin to see your ego's narrative for what it is: mere projections, not definitive truths. The life story you feel attached to becomes more like a fictional illusion—a role you're playing on the stage of your life, not what defines you at your core. This detachment allows you to separate the feeling of consciousness in your mind from your ego's narratives, allowing a deeper sense of self to emerge. That sense of self isn't preoccupied with past experiences, external validation, or future outcomes. It knows they exist, but it doesn't feel dependent on them for its existence. Rather, this sense of self is mindfully grounded in the present moment, experiencing life instance by instance without linking present events to thoughts about your past or future.

Over time, by quieting your ego and giving yourself more mental space to live in the present, mindfulness meditation allows you to develop a stable and authentic confidence. This confidence is rooted in the acceptance of yourself as you are here and now, without ruminating over past life events or doubting your ability to step into a future you. This shift in thinking allows you to approach life with greater clarity, resilience, and contentment, ultimately resulting in a more robust sense of capability.

Mindfulness meditation regulates your nervous system, calms your mind and body, and lessens self-doubt. It keeps you present and stops you from engaging in cognitive distortions through negative self-talk. By cultivating mindfulness through a regular meditation practice, you can break free from the cycle of anxious thoughts that stem from attachment to a dramatic life narrative. You can focus on the task at hand presently, without your mental capacity being diverted to thoughts about the past or future. The inner peace and self-assurance that come from mindfulness meditation can become a reliable foundation that supports you in all parts of your life, at any time and in any place.

STARTING A MEDITATION PRACTICE

Meditating on a regular basis is one of the best ways to overcome self-doubt and cultivate a lasting sense of inner confidence. For introverts especially, meditation offers a quiet space to reconnect with yourself, manage overstimulation, and restore emotional balance. Each time you meditate, you're training your brain to be more resilient. You're enabling yourself to feel a calm self-assurance as you go about your day and you're setting yourself up to stay confident the next time you're under pressure.

Starting a meditation practice is a personal journey, and there isn't a right or wrong way to do it. You don't need any special equipment, clothing, or app (though you can certainly look into any of these things if you wish; I personally have a meditation bench that I love). Here are a few steps to help you get started.

Decide on a Time. Decide what time of day you'd like to meditate. Meditating in the morning can set a positive tone for the day, allowing you to experience your day with a clearer mind and a less reactive nervous system. Meditating at night can help you unwind from the day's events, preventing you from ruminating over the current day or worrying about the next day while also improving your sleep quality. Midday meditations can lower any accumulating stress, restore your focus, and improve your performance in whatever you're doing. Ultimately, each time of day offers unique benefits, so it's worth experimenting with different times to see what works best for you.

While meditating at the same time each day isn't essential, it can help you develop a daily routine. Most people find that dedicating a specific time to meditate each day helps them stay committed by forming a habit. Other people—like me—prefer to be more spontaneous, meditating whenever they feel like it rather than at a predetermined time. Do whatever works for you.

Find a Comfortable Place. Choose a serene space. Ideally, this is somewhere quiet where you won't be disturbed. It could be a dedicated spot at home, a place at work, a seat in your car, or even somewhere outdoors. Settle into any position that feels comfortable for you, whether you're seated, lying down, in a chair, on a couch, directly on the floor, or whatnot—it really doesn't matter. The key is to find a posture that allows you to be both relaxed and alert and to breathe deeply, and one you can maintain comfortably for an extended period of time.

Start Your Session. To start off your first meditation session, take a few deep breaths to let yourself settle into the moment. Focus on each breath, noticing the sensation of the air entering and leaving your nostrils or mouth. Notice the rise and fall of your chest or the movement of your belly. As you breathe naturally, try to keep your attention on these sensations. You can count your breaths if you'd like, extending your inhales and exhales to three or four seconds each, or more. Play around with different breathing techniques to see what feels best for you.

Let Your Mind Wander. As you breathe, know that it's perfectly normal for your mind to wander. In fact, if you notice your mind wandering, that actually means you're settling into your meditation, as you now have the chance to observe your thoughts without judging them. While your mind does this, let your thoughts pass without reading into them or dwelling on them. Watch them pass by in your mind as you'd watch a car pass by on the street. Simply let your thoughts exist and be, as you gently bring your focus back to your breath. This simple act of redirecting your attention away from your thoughts and to your present experience is the heart of meditation; it builds mental resilience over time.

Build Up Your Practice. You can start by meditating for just a few minutes at a time and then work your way up to longer periods. Eventually, aim for sessions of at least ten or twenty minutes. The longer, the better.

While sticking to a daily meditation practice tends to be most beneficial, it's important to be flexible and kind to yourself. Don't stress if you can't find time every day, or even most days, to meditate. Even meditating for just one minute once a week can make a difference—it's that powerful.

Here's an easy way to meditate: Weave it into what you're already doing. Get creative and practice mindfulness during everyday activities, like while you're eating, walking, or brushing your teeth. Just by focusing on the sensations and experiences of the present moment during these activities, you're practicing a form of mindfulness meditation.

No matter how you do it, each moment you spend practicing meditation is a step toward building a more resilient, confident you. Over time, these small moments transform into profound benefits.

CONFIDENCE, DISTILLED

Acknowledge Performance Anxiety. Recognize that performance anxiety is a natural response to pressure and a common experience for many people, especially introverts.

Practice Breathwork. Use breathwork techniques to calm your mind and body during high-pressure situations.

Meditate in the Moment. Practice meditation to quiet your ego, reduce anxiety, and combat self-doubt, no matter where you are.

Build Resilience Through Regular Meditation. Meditating regularly helps build resilience, making it easier to maintain confidence under pressure.

Chapter 7

GROWING FROM REJECTION

Here's a riddle: What do you call a person who got rejected from 73 percent of the PhD programs he applied to?

I call him "me." And today you can call him "Doctor."

When I was a senior in college, I applied to eleven PhD programs, and eight of them rejected me. Fortunately, UCLA accepted me and, six years later, they were kind enough to award me a PhD.

From there on, my resume from UCLA tells an unequivocal story of success. It's meticulously manicured, boasting over forty scientific publications, seven prestigious doctoral fellowships, and many fancy research awards.

But here's what my resume doesn't say: "In his time at UCLA, Dan had over one hundred manuscripts rejected for publication, conducted more than twenty failed experiments, and was denied thousands of dollars in requested grant funding."

For every success I show to the world, a dozen rejections hide behind the scenes. But those rejections aren't for naught, nor have they held me back. They've actually pushed me forward, allowing me to become the confident person I am today.

TURNING REJECTION INTO RESILIENCE

Rejection stings. It zaps your energy. Sometimes, it makes you feel like crap. But that doesn't mean rejection is a *bad* thing. It's what you make of it.

Each rejection I've faced has given me the opportunity to reflect on my efforts and grow as a person. It's helped me see more clearly where I could improve, what I need to work on, and where my time and energy are best spent. Over time, each rejection has made me more prudent and resilient.

When you think about people who've achieved high levels of success—celebrities, professional athletes, or Nobel laureates—you don't usually think of their rejections. You probably think of their accomplishments.

Let's go back to Oprah Winfrey for a moment. She's known for developing a media empire—not for being fired from her first job as a news reporter. And Albert Einstein? He isn't remembered for the multiple teaching positions he didn't get early in his career. He's celebrated as one of the most influential scientists of all time.

Behind most successes lies a stream of rejections and for good reason. As Anthony D'Angelo aptly put it, "In order to succeed you must fail, so that you know what not to do the next time." Rejection is a natural step on the path to success. When you work through rejection by exercising your resilience, you can turn the sting of any rejection into the motivation to improve. Your resilience lets you focus on deepening and expanding your abilities, taking a forward-looking view. It enables you to accept your current circumstances and adapt to them in a self-serving way. When you draw upon your resilience, rejection doesn't fuel your self-doubt—it lessens it.

Rejection isn't the opposite of success. It's a step toward it.

Many successful people say they've not just succeeded despite rejection but *because* of it. They attribute their achievements to the resilience they built from facing rejections. Being turned down made them realize they still had work to do, and their belief in their ability to grow drove them to do that work. With the right mindset, rejection becomes a powerful motivator to persevere with self-determination.

When J. K. Rowling wrote the first Harry Potter book, she received rejection after rejection. Not one, not two, but twelve publishers rejected Rowling's first book. Now, Rowling's Harry Potter franchise has sold over 500 million books, becoming the bestselling book series in history. Reflecting on her experience with rejection, Rowling said, "I was set free, because my greatest fear had been realized, and I was still alive. . . . And so rock bottom became the solid foundation on which I rebuilt my life."

Rejection can build your resilience and your belief in yourself no matter what goal you're working toward. Widely regarded as the greatest basketball player of all time, Michael Jordan was initially cut from his high school basketball team. Instead of doubting his abilities, Jordan used this rejection as motivation to work harder and improve his skills. Rejection can feel painful, but as Jordan put it, "Learning is a gift, even when pain is your teacher." The more painful a rejection is, the more resilience you can gain from working through it.

The Beatles know this message well. They faced early rejections that nearly derailed their career. In 1962, they drove ten hours through a snowstorm to audition for Decca Records. The company famously rejected the Fab Four, emphasizing that "guitar groups are on the way out" and concluding that "The Beatles have no future in show business." Now, The Beatles reign as the bestselling band of all time.

Notice a trend here? Rejection, while painful, is often a powerful catalyst for growth. By learning from each setback and using it as a stepping stone, you can turn rejection into resilience, letting it accelerate your journey to success.

GROUNDING YOUR IDENTITY IN YOUR PROCESS

A big mistake people make when dealing with rejection is interpreting it as a threat to their sense of identity. When you invest time, effort, and emotional energy into a career, hobby, or relationship, that pursuit can become deeply intertwined with how you define yourself as an individual; it can become a core part of your identity. This contingent sense of identity can motivate you to work hard and derive meaning and purpose from your efforts. However, it also primes your mind to react to rejection with an identity crisis.

For example, if you're an aspiring musician and a record label rejects you, it's easy to panic and doubt whether you're truly destined for this career. When you feel like you've been rejected in a way that threatens your identity, it can rattle your very essence, making you question your life purpose and self-worth. In your mind, your craft and your sense of self are one and the same. A rejection of one feels like a rejection of the other.

To make rejection feel less threatening to your identity, it's important to separate your sense of self from the outcomes of your pursuits. Your identity shouldn't be attached to any outcome; it should come from the process.

Let's say you're writing a book. Instead of seeing yourself as a soon-to-be-published author, see yourself as an ambitious writer. Focus on your ability to articulate your ideas thoughtfully, hone your creative process, and demonstrate a strong work ethic. Don't define yourself by a future outcome that's largely out of your control. Define yourself by the process you're deepening right now, focusing on the qualities you're applying and developing through that process.

When you anchor your identity in your effort and determination, you gain a sense of resilience and self-worth that doesn't waver in the face of rejection. You believe in your ability to pursue your goals no matter what external feedback you receive. Focusing on the process of pursuing your goals helps you value the qualities that truly define you—your persistence, creativity, and willingness to take risks. These underlying characteristics become the core of your identity rather than the specific hobby, career, or relationship you're investing in. They make you who you are, and they exist whether you succeed or get rejected. They're the building blocks of resilience that keep your sense of identity—and your confidence—unwavering in the face of rejection. The bottom line? Detach yourself from outcomes and attach yourself to the personality traits and values you channel when you pursue a meaningful goal.

When you derive your identity from the process and not the outcome, you cultivate a sense of intrinsic motivation. You feel more driven by your passion and purpose rather than the need for external approval. After all, rejection is inherently a form of external feedback. Compared to extrinsic motivation, intrinsic motivation is more sustainable, fulfilling, and resilient. Because it comes from within you, intrinsic motivation isn't shaken by external feedback. It helps you interpret each experience on the way toward your goals—whether positive or negative—as an opportunity to validate your inner characteristics and affirm your identity as someone attached to a journey, not wedded to any single outcome.

Identifying with your process transforms rejection from a threat to your self-worth into an opportunity to reaffirm who you truly are. It also allows you to consider what you can learn from the rejection. As you identify with your process instead of your outcome, you validate your inner characteristics and naturally become more growth-oriented. You focus on how you can develop your current weaknesses, capitalize on your strengths, and take one more step toward realizing your potential. You step into the future rather than stagnate in the present.

When you separate your identity from outcomes, rejection no longer feels personal. Rather, it's just neutral information. Grounding your identity in your process enables you to respond to rejection levelheadedly. It encourages you to affirm your inner self-worth—that you're a hardworking, creative, passionate, empathic, artistic person, or whichever traits you view as central to your process. It enables you to demonstrate those traits in how you respond to rejection. Those traits allow you to pursue your goals and are a source of inner resilience that help you stay confident no matter what outcomes you face.

REJECTION IS AN UNTAPPED GIFT

Rejection isn't personal—it's just feedback.

Rejection isn't a judgment of your potential; it's a valuable opportunity to gain feedback and grow. It's a natural part of the journey toward success that allows you to see what you need to work on. The more you adopt this perspective, the more you can see rejection as an untapped gift. Rejection is what you make of it, and you can often turn it into a self-serving advantage.

Time and time again, rejection doesn't just fuel growth; it spurs innovation. Many artists, entrepreneurs, and musicians have used rejection as a catalyst to push the boundaries of their work, elevate their current efforts to the next level, or try something different altogether.

In 1919, Walt Disney was fired from his first animation job on the basis that he "lacked imagination and had no good ideas." After being fired, Disney doubled down on his identity as an animator and founded Laugh-O-Gram Studio, where he experimented with a variety of animation and storytelling styles. When Laugh-O-Gram went bankrupt, Walt Disney still didn't question his identity as an animator. He embraced it even further. He took what he learned from his experience running the studio, persevered in following his passion, and founded the Disney Brothers Studio. That studio is known today as The Walt Disney Company, and it's worth over $200 billion. Disney's rejections led him to create some of the world's most influential pillars of modern pop culture and entertainment.

By maintaining his identity as an animator in the face of rejection, Walt Disney found intrinsic motivation in others' denials of his efforts and developed his resilience. He transformed his early setbacks into opportunities for innovation. He didn't take rejection as a personal attack on his potential; he let it guide him toward realizing his potential more fully. His ability to adapt, experiment, and believe in his abilities set the foundation for The Walt Disney Company's enduring legacy.

By reframing rejection from an identity threat into an opportunity to affirm who you really are, you can transform rejection into a powerful catalyst for growth. Embracing rejection as a learning experience that refines your process will deepen your confidence. Each rejection you face and overcome adds to your reservoir of resilience, proving to yourself that you won't just tolerate adversity—you'll grow stronger from it. You'll see how rejection doesn't stop you in your tracks. Rather, it gives you an opportunity to validate your inner traits and values, letting you feel more confident in your ability to overcome rejection in the future. As you become more accustomed to navigating challenges and emerging stronger from them, the fear of rejection fades. In its place emerges a more resilient sense of self-assurance and determination.

Every rejection deepens your reservoir of resilience.

MAKING REJECTION LESS PAINFUL

It can be counterintuitive to imagine that confidence can come from rejection. Most people feel *less* confident after being rejected because it feels like someone else is telling them they can't achieve their goals. It's perfectly normal to feel awful after experiencing rejection. Rejection can be intensely painful, and feeling pain for a short while is often an inevitable part of the experience. The problem arises when people unknowingly extend this pain and let it linger in their minds long term. When this happens, the painful aftermath of rejection turns into lingering self-doubt.

To prevent rejection from fueling self-doubt, you need to process it healthily and set yourself up to grow from it. The best way to do this is by understanding the psychology behind why rejection feels painful and knowing how to keep this pain short-lived.

Rejection triggers three main psychological processes that feel painful and lower your confidence in the short term.

First, rejection can take a toll on your self-esteem. When you attach your identity to your outcomes, rejection can feel like a personal affront, leading you to question your worth and abilities. When a person or organization doesn't accept you, it can feel like they're saying that who you are as a person isn't enough. This hit to your self-esteem can cause negative self-talk that keeps you feeling weighed down. It's common for people to bring themselves down after rejection with thoughts like "I'm not good enough" or "I'll never succeed," and these thoughts reflect self-doubt that erodes your self-esteem and, in turn, your confidence.

Second, rejection causes emotional distress and a sense of suffering as it activates the same neural pathways in your brain that light up when you experience physical pain. This distress can be intense, bringing down your mood, ambition, and energy. When you enter this state of mind, your confidence naturally stagnates.

Third, rejection can induce crippling anxiety and strip away your confidence by priming your mind to anticipate and fear being rejected again in the future. This anticipatory anxiety can make you hesitant to take risks or put yourself in situations where you might face rejection again. Your self-doubt leads to inaction. You might start avoiding any and all opportunities that could lead to failure out of an abundance of caution to protect your fragile self-esteem and to soothe your anxiety. This avoidance prevents you from challenging yourself and growing, all the while reinforcing your feelings of inadequacy.

Rejection threatens your confidence in these ways when your mind creates narratives about what rejection means. The key word in that sentence? *Narratives.* The mind has a way of engaging in cognitive distortions, taking events that happen in your life and blowing their significance out of proportion. These cognitive distortions are, yet again, the ego speaking—yes, that same ego who hates calmness and craves drama.

Two cognitive distortions that arise from rejection are overgeneralizing and catastrophizing. These distorted ways of thinking create unfounded self-doubt that seeps into your mind like slow-acting poisons. They feel like your own true thoughts, but they're really just a load of nonsense. By understanding these two cognitive distortions and noticing their pull, you can realize when they're happening in the moment and lift yourself out of them. This process is particularly beneficial for introverts, whose introspective nature makes them prone to dwelling on negative experiences more intensely. Calling out your cognitive distortions, however, can nip this brooding in the bud. That keeps the pain of rejection short-lived and lets you take your confidence back into your own hands.

Cognitive Distortion #1: Overgeneralizing Rejection

Overgeneralization is the first type of cognitive distortion that creates self-doubt in the face of rejection. When you overgeneralize, you draw broad, sweeping conclusions from a single situation where you've been rejected and apply them to all similar situations, assuming that rejection is your future from here on out. For example, if you apply for a job and don't get an offer, you might start believing that you're not employable at all. Or if you experience a romantic rejection, you might tell yourself something like "No one will ever love me." These sweeping statements are not based on objective reality but on an overblown emotional response. They're distorted ways of thinking.

Overgeneralizing is toxic for confidence because it creates exaggerated self-doubt that easily turns into feelings of incapability and worthlessness. When people believe that rejection is inevitable because of their inadequacy, they might stop trying altogether. When they do go after a goal, they do it with a low amount of effort and enthusiasm, feeling like it's not worth investing time and energy into something destined to fail. Their main aim isn't to succeed; it's to conserve any amount of self-esteem they have left by never putting themselves out there. This mindset creates a self-fulfilling prophecy where someone's belief that rejection is inevitable ultimately leads them to face more rejection. Once that cycle starts, it becomes hard to end.

Cognitive Distortion #2: Catastrophizing Rejection

Just as some people may overgeneralize a rejection, others may also catastrophize it. Catastrophizing is a cognitive distortion where you assume the worst possible outcome from a rejection. It's when your mind spins down a rabbit hole of negativity, making the rejection seem far worse than it actually is and making you feel like you're powerless to do anything about it.

Catastrophizing is dangerous for confidence because it makes you feel as though your most feared outcomes are inevitable, as though they're written in stone. It makes you feel helpless. For example, after getting rejected from a job, someone who catastrophizes might think, "I'll never find a job, and I'll end up homeless." When you catastrophize, you develop an exaggerated perception of the consequences of rejection, and it feels as though your ability to exercise resilience doesn't exist.

REJECTION IS INEVITABLE—BUT ITS AFTERMATH ISN'T

By recognizing and addressing cognitive distortions, you can keep the pain of rejection short-lived and maintain your confidence. Understand that rejection is a natural part of the journey and use it as a tool for growth so you can emerge stronger and more resilient from it. The best way to do this is, once again, to separate your identity from your outcomes. It's to view rejection as a reflection of your current abilities rather than as a signal of your potential.

When you take rejection personally, you view it as evidence that you're unworthy of success and start to believe that you don't have the potential to succeed in the future. This is when you begin overgeneralizing and catastrophizing.

Conversely, when you view rejection as a reflection of the effort you've just put forth, you understand that the rejection doesn't say anything about you as a person. You realize that it signals there is more work to be done. You see rejection as a stepping stone along the way to success, knowing that you can grow and improve for next time.

After any rejection, take time to reflect on your ultimate goal and reevaluate which smaller goals can get you there. Set new, smaller goals that reignite your motivation and provide a clear path forward. By redirecting your focus away from your ultimate goal toward step-by-step objectives that feel more attainable, you can lessen the sting of rejection and feel more capable.

Rejection isn't a verdict on your worth. It's proof you're pushing past your comfort zone.

For example, if you're applying for jobs but face rejection after an interview, set smaller goals to prepare yourself for the next opportunity. Set goals to revise your resume, take a skill-development workshop, or form a new connection with someone in your field. When you break down the larger task of securing a job into manageable parts, you can view each of those parts as a micro-goal. Build up momentum and confidence by achieving these micro-goals.

Each step forward, no matter how small, reinforces your belief in your ability to succeed. It helps you find new growth in the wake of rejection. Being proactive in this way gives you an empowering mindset, shifting your focus from what went wrong to what you can do next. It prevents you from catastrophizing and reminds you that setbacks are temporary and surmountable.

Rejection is a guarantee in life. It's an inevitable byproduct of expressing who you are, saying how you feel, and going after your goals. From the day you're born to the day you die, there will be people who turn you down and pass you over. While rejection can be deeply painful and unsettling, accepting its inevitability and learning to cope with it is crucial for developing confidence through adaptive resilience.

Dismissing rejection isn't the solution. Sure, ignoring rejection may feel good temporarily, but when you dismiss rejection, you deny yourself an opportunity for growth and reflection. Rejection can help you become more aware of your shortcomings or show you what you need to work on to improve your next efforts. People who deal with rejection in a healthy way listen to what each rejection has to offer them without taking it personally.

By viewing rejection as an opportunity for learning, you can use it to self-reflect without creating self-doubt. This approach keeps the pain of rejection short-lived while opening the door to deeper confidence. It lets you take more of your life story into your own hands, moving forward with a stronger belief in your ability to pursue your goals.

CONFIDENCE, DISTILLED

Accept Rejection as Normal. Understand that rejection is an inevitable part of life and a natural step on the journey toward success.

Overcome and Grow. Successful people don't dodge rejection; they overcome it and grow from it. And so can you.

Don't Take It Personally. Rejection doesn't say anything about your abilities or worth.

Anchor Your Identity in the Process. Define yourself by your drive, resilience, and values, not by the outcomes of your efforts.

Learn and Reflect. Use rejection as an opportunity for self-reflection and personal growth, leveraging your introspective tendencies to foster resilience and confidence.

Chapter 8

RETHINKING TRAGEDY

When I turned twenty-five, I started losing use of my hands. I woke up one day barely able to tie my own shoes, and it wasn't long until I transitioned to slip-on shoes without laces. I felt my livelihood as an academic and writer start to slip away as I lost my ability to write or type. Ideas were stagnating in my mind because I couldn't get them down onto paper. Even playing table tennis—my lifelong passion—became a painful struggle as simply gripping the paddle was almost unbearable.

It was one of the scariest times of my life. I was only twenty-five and yet already experiencing the debilitations of aging, as if I'd jumped into the body of an eighty-five-year-old with advanced arthritis. Cerebral palsy ages you before you know it.

For all my life until then, I'd worked on rehabilitating the physical abilities I lost from my brain injury at birth. I'd developed my abilities and minimized my feeling of disability, pushing the boundaries of what seemed possible. I'd become a brown belt in karate, an internationally ranked table tennis player, and was on my way toward receiving a PhD. I'd carved my own path in life and defined for myself the parameters of what I could do.

Losing the use of my hands, I felt those parameters caving in and my abilities slipping away. I was terrified by the thought of being unable to work, pursue any of my passions, or care for myself. My job as an academic, my efforts as an athlete, my independence as an adult—these were the fiber of my essence. They were how I defined myself, and feeling them slip away felt like losing the most fundamental parts of my identity. I felt helpless.

This experience was a stark wake-up call. It forced me to confront the fragility of my body as it aged prematurely and reignited my determination to author my own story once again. From this scare, I committed myself to restarting the rehabilitative therapy I knew too well as a child, accepting that this time around, I wasn't working to expand my body's abilities; I was fighting to keep Father Time from taking them away.

In the face of this adversity, I discovered a deeper well of resilience within myself. I relearned the importance of adaptability, self-care, and the relentless pursuit of my passions. My experience taught me that while my physical abilities may change over time, the essence of who I am—my determination, creativity, and drive—remains steadfast.

As Viktor Frankl wisely said, "When we are no longer able to change a situation, we are challenged to change ourselves." My struggle wasn't just about dealing with physical loss; it was about rethinking my identity and looking for new ways to define myself beyond my physical capabilities.

Still in my twenties, I shifted my perspective from seeing myself as a young adult to considering my future as an aging one. While I'd long felt like my days in occupational therapy were behind me, I started them up again with sessions twice a week. I realized that I could no longer take for granted the physical abilities I'd worked so hard in the past to develop. I'd have to continually work to maintain them, understanding that these abilities are only the surface of who I truly am.

PILLARS OF CONFIDENCE TAKEN FOR GRANTED

Personal tragedies happen throughout life. Inevitably, you'll go through significant events that disrupt your sense of normalcy, eroding a feeling of comfort you didn't know you could lose. These events can challenge your resilience, catching you off guard, sending you into a storm of despair and worry, and stripping away your confidence.

We often live our lives with an unconscious sense of security, assuming that the abilities, relationships, roles, talents, and freedoms we have now will always be there with us. These are the hidden pillars of confidence that support our sense of self. They give our lives clear meaning and purpose, reinforce the identities we present to the world, and allow us to pursue any goals and pleasures we wish. Rarely do we pause to consider how integral these pillars are to our psychological well-being—until they disappear.

Know your pillars of confidence: the abilities, relationships, and roles that give you meaning and sustain your confidence.

Consider the ability to type on a laptop, tablet, or phone. For most people in developed countries, it's an automatic action performed without a second thought, just like it had become for me after years of work in occupational therapy. My ability to type became a cornerstone of my identity as an academic and writer, allowing me to thrive intellectually despite feeling otherwise limited physically. The difficulty I faced with my hands left me with a profound sense of loss and anxiety, eroding the foundation of agency and comfort I once relied on. It was a wake-up call to how much of my confidence rested on my intellectual and professional activities and a stark reminder of how I'd taken for granted that my hands could, and I thought always would, function. Losing this ability, even temporarily, felt like losing a core part of myself.

It's not just physical abilities that we take for granted. Social, financial, and emotional experiences are also significant pillars of confidence. The end of a relationship, a layoff from a job, or the loss of a loved one can all have a devastating impact on your ability to believe in yourself. Personal tragedies can expose the hidden pillars of confidence that you didn't even know existed, pillars that support you in your everyday routines and larger ambitions.

Personal tragedies can expose hidden pillars of confidence that you didn't even know existed.

Tragic events disrupt the psychological resources we subconsciously rely on to operate with self-assurance and agency. They upend our lives and goals, revealing to us what we care about most. They can strip away the structures of support that underlie much of our confidence, showing us what we've taken for granted all along. They reveal our pillars of confidence.

RECOGNIZING YOUR PILLARS OF CONFIDENCE

When something disrupts your pillars of confidence, you're forced to confront the fragility of your existence. But this disruption also invites you to ask yourself: *Where does my confidence really come from?*

Recognizing your hidden pillars of confidence is a crucial step toward restoring your confidence in the face of tragedy or adversity. When you understand the foundations upon which your self-assurance rests, you gain an inner clarity that supports you through any experience you face. Much of the distress and despair people feel during tough times comes not from the events themselves but from a lack of self-understanding. They don't understand why they really feel so lousy, and that lack of understanding makes them feel even lousier. Getting in touch with the inner workings of your mind makes tough times more manageable. It allows you to see clearly which basic needs and goals your suffering stems from and which emotions you're feeling.

Identifying your pillars of confidence begins with introspection and self-awareness. Start by reflecting on the activities, relationships, and roles that bring you the most joy, satisfaction, and sense of achievement. Consider the aspects of your life where you feel proud, capable, and valued. These are often the areas where your confidence is most deeply rooted.

Ask yourself:

- What do I do that makes me feel capable, competent, or accomplished?

- Which relationships in my life give me the deepest sense of love, support, and belonging?
- Which parts of my identity am I most proud of?
- What goals or ambitions in my life matter most to me?
- What personal strengths have carried me through difficult times before?
- Where and when do I feel most like myself—authentic, confident, and at ease?

Reflecting on these questions can give you clarity into your pillars of confidence. Think about the physical and mental abilities, as well as the social, emotional, and financial resources, that allow you to pursue and maintain these sources of confidence.

Another effective approach to discovering your pillars of confidence is to pay attention to your emotional responses during times of stress or adversity. When faced with a challenge, try to pinpoint what exactly you fear losing or what thought causes you the most anxiety, discomfort, or pain. These reactions often point to the underlying pillars of your confidence as your mind recognizes the risk of losing them. If you're an introvert by nature, use your introversion to your advantage by listening to what your inner world has to say. More often than not, it already holds the answers.

One exercise you can do is to list out all the times you've felt a sense of loss, anxiety, or frustration in the past few months or years. For each experience, identify what emotions come up for you and what imaginary "worst-case scenario" your mind may have ruminated on. By understanding these emotional cues, you can identify the core goals and roles that support your confidence.

Resilience begins when you stop taking your pillars of confidence for granted.

When you understand your pillars of confidence, you gain three strengths of adaptive resilience:

1. **Gratitude.** You become aware of the cherished abilities, relationships, roles, talents, and freedoms you have right now that you take for granted. By appreciating these hidden assets while you have them, you can draw upon them fully and build up your self-esteem by recognizing and valuing their existence.
2. **Control Over Your Mind.** By understanding your pillars of confidence, you gain control over how your mind works during difficult times. Reflecting on your pillars of confidence helps you realize that you almost definitely have more pillars than you thought, providing you with a more flexible resilience. It allows you to map out your pillars of confidence and see how many pillars support your life. This process can be a powerful exercise as it helps you control which specific pillar of confidence your mind focuses on at any given moment.

   Typically, when a difficult life event occurs, one pillar is threatened more than the others. For example, a breakup threatens a relationship pillar, a job loss erodes a financial pillar, and an injury impacts a physical pillar. The mind's natural response is to hyperfocus on whichever pillar is threatened at the moment, which feels painful and demoralizing. However, recognizing the variety of pillars you possess allows you to shift your focus away from your threatened pillar to another pillar. When one pillar is threatened, you can draw strength from a different pillar. For instance, during a breakup, you can focus on a valued hobby or friendship to regain a sense of agency and capability.

3. **New Pillars.** A third strength of resilience you gain from understanding the pillars of your confidence is the ability to develop new pillars in your life. You can transform moments of tragedy into opportunities for growth.

   Personal tragedies are transformative experiences that force you to reassess your life and question the sources of your confidence. While it's easy to hyperfocus on whichever pillar is currently under threat, remember that this time presents a hidden opportunity: to strengthen that pillar back to health or to develop a new pillar altogether.

   Challenging times allow you to bring to light the pillars of confidence you once took for granted, emerging with stronger, more resilient foundations. If you can restore the pillar of confidence that's currently suffering, you can stop taking it for granted in the future and start appreciating it. You can become aware of it and invest in it, just as I did by working on my ability to use my hands through occupational therapy. I no longer take my ability to use my hands for granted. Rather, I work to maintain that ability, spending time stretching and exercising my hands every day. In doing so, I realize I now have the knowledge and drive to heal my hands when they need healing. That perspective makes me more resilient and feel more in control over my future. It transforms anxiety into agency. I've used a tragic time in my life to develop a deeper, more enduring sense of self-assurance that'll help me withstand future adversities.

   If you can't strengthen a suffering pillar, you can build a new pillar. Painful experiences often serve as catalysts for introspection and exploration, but only if you let them. By introspecting on your loss and allowing yourself to move on from it, you can heal and find a renewed sense of confidence, direction, and even purpose in life.

Heartbreak taught me this last lesson the hard way. Remember my Valentine's Day story from Chapter 2? Well, let's cut to that breakup.

When I got my heart broken for the first time, it felt like a crack had split through the foundation of who I was. I felt unmotivated to get out of bed each day and fell into despair. I lost the energy and drive to go about my life and enjoy the things I normally did.

After a few weeks of despair, this breakup became one of the most positive turning points in my life. All I could think about was the pain in my romantic life, and I wanted to channel my pain into something fruitful that gave me a sense of control and achievement. In this dark place, I started to help other people write their online dating profiles. I figured that while my own love life was in the dumps, at least I could help others with theirs.

I went all in and started my own company to bring this idea to life: The Match Lab LLC. Through this company, I used my expertise on the psychology of attraction and relationships and my experience as a writer to help people find love. I had no experience running a business or coaching clients, but I threw myself into this project, knowing it was what I needed to heal myself. It allowed me to establish a new pillar of confidence in my life. Within a few days of working on my company, I felt a newfound sense of energy, purpose, and direction. I was back.

PROGRESS COMES AND GOES

Making progress in life—whether on your personal growth, a hobby, a relationship, or your career—often forms the basis of confidence, giving you pillars that can last for decades. But progress isn't guaranteed to last forever; it's like a rug that can be pulled out from under you at any time.

You can't always know whether the progress you make in life will stay with you, so you can't always control which pillars of confidence you'll have at your disposal at any given moment. However, you *can* control how you respond to shifts in your pillars as progress comes and goes. The choice to find new pillars is always yours.

FINDING ENERGY WITHIN PAIN

My first breakup shifted my pillars of confidence, giving me a new identity as an entrepreneur and dating coach. It was exciting to step into this new role and grow from it as I took pride in creating my own brand, felt a sense of purpose in helping clients with their dating lives, and developed new skill sets along the way. These feelings, in turn, took me from a state of apathy and defeat into a place of zeal and confidence.

Starting a business is a radical way to cope with any kind of loss—and one I wouldn't recommend—but it served me well at the time. One of the main reasons why personal tragedy can zap your confidence is that tragedy drains your energy levels. When you're in any kind of pain, whether physical or emotional, the mind's natural response is to retreat and withdraw. It's common to feel lethargic and unmotivated during difficult times.

To reignite your confidence after a tragedy, you need to make your mind remember why it craves confidence in the first place: to help you express yourself and achieve goals. Even when tragedy makes you feel despair, depression, and fatigue, your mind always wants an outlet for its focus. It's wired to focus on something at all times. When your mind lacks any external focus during hard times, it can feel like your mind is eating itself alive, fixating on your pain and suffering endlessly.

Giving your mind a relevant outlet to occupy itself with helps you regain energy. Because your mind is no longer retreating into itself and focusing intently on your pain, the impact of your tragedy starts to feel lighter. Goals begin to feel worth pursuing again, and your ability to feel confident revs up once more.

That's what my dating coaching company did for me—it allowed me to regain my energy and ambition by channeling the pain of my tragedy (heartbreak) into a relevant outlet (helping others find love). Just when I felt the least sense of control over my own love life, I regained a similar feeling of control by helping others with theirs. Once my mind shifted focus from my internal suffering to this external outlet, I realized there was a great deal of energy hidden within my pain. It was just a matter of unlocking it.

> **Every emotion carries energy. Decide how to use it.**

When personal tragedies have you feeling lost and apathetic, you can regain your ability to feel confident again by finding energy within your pain. Start by allowing yourself to fully experience and acknowledge your emotions. Suppressing feelings of sadness, anger, or frustration may feel good in the short term, but it'll backfire in the long term by draining your energy further and making it harder to move forward. Instead, accept these emotions as a normal and natural response to your situation. And remember that you're not your emotions; they don't define you. They're just temporary sensations you experience, offering you a form of energy in the moment.

Every emotion you experience, whether positive or negative, is a powerful source of energy and motivation. Emotions are "goal-oriented cognitions." That means they're closely tied to your basic needs and desires. They influence how you perceive and respond to situations that matter to you.

Positive emotions like joy, excitement, and love can energize you, making you feel enthusiastic and capable of achieving your goals. These emotions drive you to be social and engage with others. Negative emotions like sadness, anger, and frustration can drive you to feel apathetic, socially withdrawn, or outraged with pumping veins and a vendetta, but they can also be harnessed as positively potent motivators when you give them an appropriate outlet.

When you channel negative feelings into constructive outlets, they can fuel your resilience and give you a sense of ambition and, eventually, a sense of achievement. Emotions like anger and frustration arouse the body and can provide you with energy to start a new sport, exercise plan, or fitness goal. Emotions like sadness and loneliness, meanwhile, slow down your thoughts and behaviors, leading you to introspect and reflect. This slowing down can allow you to process complex emotions and understand your experiences profoundly. Finding a creative or artistic outlet for these emotions can lead you to channel this slow energy into a feeling of achievement. Vincent van Gogh, for example, famously suffered from depression and channeled his emotional turmoil into his work.

Starting any kind of pursuit in the aftermath of tragedy can give you a clearer sense of direction during unclear times. For example, if you've experienced a personal loss, volunteering or supporting others facing similar challenges can be both therapeutic and empowering. When you start working on something you view as valuable, simply the act of starting that work can muster up the energy and ambition you need to continue onward with it. Pursuing any kind of project can allow you to process and release emotions, and that release is what lets you feel the energy hidden within them.

It's common to think that you need a certain level of clear energy to go out and do something. But often, deciding to do something is what allows you to discover hidden sources of energy within. Discovering and pursuing those sources of energy can pull you out of post-tragedy rut, allowing you to emerge even stronger than when you entered.

HEALING FROM TRAGEDY BUILDS INNER PILLARS OF CONFIDENCE

Going through a tough breakup didn't just send me down an entrepreneurial path; it also encouraged me to start healing myself from within. My breakup was the impetus I needed to start going to therapy. While launching a business provided a great external focus for my mind, I knew I was in a psychological state of pain beyond what I could resolve on my own. Focusing my attention inward would be essential to becoming the best, most resilient, and most confident version of myself in the long term.

Personal tragedies have a way of revealing the inner turmoil of your mind. They expose the parts of yourself you need to work on to heal your traumas, resolve your lingering insecurities, and quiet your self-doubt. They strip away the conscious defenses your mind places upon suppressed thoughts and feelings, allowing these emotions to surface. These revelations feel especially intense for introverts as they amplify the volume of your inner dialogue.

Confronting the ugly parts of yourself can cause great pain, shame, and fear. It's natural to want to run away from difficult feelings. But the reality is that pushing negative thoughts aside won't help you feel any better in the long term. The only way to improve your feelings is by healing the psychological wounds that drive those negative thoughts.

That's where therapy comes in. No matter where you are in life, I encourage everyone to try therapy if it's accessible to you. Working with a trained mental health professional can help you develop a deeper, more authentic, and more resilient base of confidence by healing the wounded parts of your mind that fill you with chronic self-doubt. Mental wounds can accumulate throughout life at such a low level that you're not even aware of them. Over time, these wounds add up, creating distorted patterns of thinking that hold you back in your everyday life. And if therapy isn't available, there are still other ways to begin healing—through trusted friends, religious or spiritual leaders, journaling, support groups, or self-help resources. No matter how you go about it, the goal is the same: to untangle the pain that holds you back, deepen your self-awareness, and rebuild a stronger, more secure foundation for your mind.

Healing turns wounds into wisdom, pain into power.

Personally, my experience in therapy taught me what it means to be truly confident by being there for myself. Processing my breakup gave me a clear understanding of what it means to love myself, whether or not I have someone else by my side to make me feel loved. By providing a structured space for deep introspection and self-exploration, therapy helped me understand my needs and build a more resilient sense of self.

Within all pain lies the potential for healing, growth, and a more resilient belief in yourself. Personal tragedy is often the impetus needed to reflect inward, to rethink what really matters to you, and to turn the life you've been living into the life you'd like to live.

When tragedy strikes and you feel yourself suffering from it, listen to that suffering. It might just teach you more about yourself than you knew existed. Embrace the pain as a catalyst for growth. Allow yourself to feel, process, and heal. Use this period of introspection to rebuild your inner pillars of confidence stronger than before.

CONFIDENCE, DISTILLED

Learn from Tragedy. Personal tragedy can push you to reassess your self-worth and build resilience, helping you understand yourself and grow.

Identify Your Pillars of Confidence. Recognize the abilities, relationships, and roles that give you a sense of meaning in life and underlie your core sense of confidence.

Find Energy Within Pain. Channel negative emotions into productive outlets, using them to regain motivation and confidence during challenging times.

Reflect and Heal. Develop resilience by addressing and healing inner wounds through therapeutic guidance and self-reflection.

Build New Pillars of Confidence. Use personal tragedy as a catalyst to cultivate new skills, hobbies, or relationships that reinforce your overall sense of confidence.

KEY #3

INQUISITIVE SELF-DISCOVERY

Chapter 9

RECONNECTING WITH YOUR INNER CHILD

Throughout my childhood, therapy putty was everywhere. If you're unfamiliar with it, imagine Play-Doh on steroids. While Play-Doh is designed for fun, putty is designed for work. Play-Doh is soft and molds effortlessly into cool shapes; putty is intentionally stiff and challenges your hands, giving them a workout as you knead it with effort.

Putty was the centerpiece of my time in occupational therapy. I'd meet with my therapist, get my hands stretched out, do a few exercises, and then play with putty. My therapist's office was filled with dozens of putty containers, each a different color indicating a different level of firmness. The firmer the putty, the tougher it was to knead. Advancing to a new color felt like graduating to a new grade in occupational therapy. It was exhilarating.

As a child, I spent so much time in occupational and physical therapy that activities like working with putty became a form of playtime. For me, occupational therapy was where we worked on my hands, and physical therapy was where we worked on the rest of my body. Between the two, I sat on giant exercise balls, threw Frisbees, played games of catch, did yoga, and drew pictures with crayons. While my friends were with other kids out playing sports or at home playing video games, I was often balancing on a half-dome exercise ball while playing catch with a physical therapist seven times my age.

Back then, I felt like I was missing out on the free time that other children had for play. In hindsight, though, I now appreciate the variety of formative experiences I had growing up with cerebral palsy. Playtime wasn't just with friends, family, and my karate class; it was also with physical therapists, occupational therapists, speech therapists, physiatrists, neurologists, and orthopedic surgeons. These adults didn't just treat me; they joked with me, cheered me on when I mastered a new movement, and turned tedious exercises into games. Through their encouragement, I discovered who I was and how I could express myself physically and intellectually. I set goals, challenged myself, and grew from my efforts, all while having fun.

In high school, I took up pottery and found a love for crafting ceramics by hand. Working with clay took me back to the days of kneading putty in occupational therapy and gave me the freedom to invent, design, and create. I made vases and bowls, painting them freely and firing them to a glossy finish in kilns. Pottery-making became a passion, and I even became the president of my high school's ceramics club. Every Thursday after school, I reconnected with my younger self and simply played, becoming immersed in the process and losing track of time and space.

Playtime, as I learned, was more than an escape. It was a vital part of my development, helping me grow, express myself, and discover my strengths. By reconnecting with my inner child and embracing the spirit of play as an adult, I've unlocked new levels of self-discovery and confidence. And so can you.

Playtime is more than an escape. It's a vital part of psychological development—for kids *and* adults.

PLAY IS A FUNDAMENTAL HUMAN NEED

Playtime isn't just an excuse to have fun; it's one of the most quintessential expressions of being human. It's a fundamental need that allows children to develop into fully functioning adults—physically, socially, and emotionally. And it doesn't stop there. Play provides people of all ages with the psychological experiences they need to develop self-confidence.

Think back to your favorite childhood playtime activities—whether it was chasing your friends during a game of tag, building castles with blocks, spending hours on a puzzle, drawing with chalk, crayons, or colored pencils, getting messy with fingerpaints and glitter, climbing around a jungle gym, or playing some kind of make-believe with friends. In any form they took, these moments of play were crucial to nurturing the social and cognitive abilities you need to develop confidence. Visionary child psychologist Jean Piaget believed that play is how children make sense of the world. It's through play that children explore ideas, experiment with their environment, and discover how things work.

Playtime hones the young mind for developing confidence by allowing a child to explore their abilities, take risks, and recover from setbacks in an environment that's filled with curiosity. Through play, children experience moments of success, learn from their mistakes, and build a sense of competence and mastery over their actions, realizing that they're capable of achieving goals and shaping the world around them. This process helps them develop self-esteem and resilience, allowing them to believe in their abilities.

While playtime during childhood lays a foundation for entering adulthood with a good sense of confidence, the benefits of play don't stop when you turn eighteen, or any age for that matter. Unfortunately, many cultures devalue play in adulthood, viewing it as infantile and a waste of time. This view isn't just harmful to mental health; it's also entirely false.

OPPORTUNITIES FOR PLAY ARE EVERYWHERE

Here's how psychologists define play: any activity that's intrinsically motivated, freely chosen, and enjoyable. Let's break that definition down.

First, play is *intrinsically motivated.* This means that the desire to engage in play comes from a drive within you, not from some kind of external pressure or reward. People play simply because it brings them personal satisfaction and joy. They don't have any other incentive.

Second, play is *freely chosen.* In other words, it's voluntary. This means that people choose to play of their own free will, and they can stop playing at any time they wish. Nobody is forcing or pressuring them to play.

Third, play is *enjoyable.* It's first and foremost about having fun, experiencing pleasure, and feeling fulfilled.

When you think about play in this way, it's easy to see that opportunities for play are all around us. It's just a matter of recognizing those opportunities and taking them up.

You likely engage in play more often than you realize. Perhaps you immerse yourself in craft projects like knitting, painting, gardening, or woodworking. You might enjoy home improvement and DIY projects or love cooking and baking, experimenting with new recipes. Maybe you stay active through sports, hiking, dance, or yoga, or have game nights with friends, playing board, card, or video games. You might stimulate your creative mind with crosswords, puzzles, chess, books, journaling, or musical instruments. Or you might simply enjoy spending time being silly with your pet each day.

If any of these activities resonate with you, think about how they fit with that definition of play. Chances are, you'll see how each activity is intrinsically motivated, freely chosen, and enjoyable. That's play.

PLAY CHANNELS YOUR INNER CHILD

For most adults, play provides some of life's most valued moments and memories. It makes life fun and makes you feel alive. For introverts, play can provide a meaningful way to recharge and engage in self-discovery without the overstimulation that can come from more socially draining activities.

Playtime activities are creative, expressive, and rewarding. They induce a flow state, where often you feel so immersed in what you're doing that you lose track of time or your surroundings. Play offers a space for you to think freely, take risks, and explore new possibilities without self-consciousness or the fear of failure. It stimulates your brain, keeping it flexible and adaptable. It makes you feel expansive, less bound by the rules and expectations of the world. Ultimately, in these ways, play boosts your confidence and channels your inner child.

> **Play boosts your confidence by channeling your inner child—a part of you that's full of joy and free from self-doubt.**

Your inner child is the part of your psyche that embodies the qualities of a young child, uninfluenced by the outer world. Everyone has an inner child, regardless of their age. Your inner child is your source of curiosity, spontaneity, creativity, and wonder. It's the pure joy you feel when living in the moment, unaware of time passing by or the demands of the world around you. It's a part of you that's free from self-doubt.

Because your inner child is free from self-doubt, it's a rich source of inner confidence. The beauty of your inner child is that it's always within you, lending you a mindset you can channel at any time. For most people, though, the problem is that their inner child is chronically suppressed as they go about their lives acting like adults—and they need to rediscover it.

As people preoccupy their minds with the roles, pressures, and expectations of adulthood, they play less. They lose touch with their inner child and even deny its existence, seeing childhood and playfulness as immature and not part of the script of adult life. This detachment makes life feel like a performance, making it harder to channel a lasting sense of confidence from within.

ADULTHOOD IS A PERFORMANCE

In the words of renowned sociologist Erving Goffman, "We are all just actors trying to control and manage our public image. We act based on how others might see us."

Back in the 1950s, Goffman came up with a clever metaphor that life is just one big theater stage. According to Goffman, people are actors on that stage, performing roles in front of an audience. These roles—like being an employee, a student, a parent, an athlete, or a friend—are various identities you take on in different contexts. Your "audience" is anyone observing your performance, reacting to how well you fulfill these roles.

As young children, we have few roles to perform. We're mostly free to think, feel, and behave as we desire, expressing ourselves without feeling restricted or concerned with expectations. We live from a place of our inner child.

The more we focus on performing roles, the more we suppress our inner child. We feel more concerned with social expectations and other people's reactions to us, and we doubt ourselves as a result. This creates a paradox:

On one hand, taking on new roles as we grow helps define our place in the world and can boost self-worth when we meet societal expectations. We feel mature, valued, and capable. On the other hand, stepping into these roles too much makes adulthood feel like a continuous performance. It can make you feel like you're stuck onstage, acting out a script that isn't fully yours.

Spending too much time and energy on performing roles pressures you to adapt your thoughts and behaviors to fit societal standards. While fulfilling roles and responsibilities is necessary for the realities of adult life, it's equally important to honor the inner child within you. Constantly performing roles can lead you to lose touch with your genuine self, masking your inner child—your source of innate joy, creativity, and unfiltered confidence.

The opposite of play isn't work. It's self-doubt.

REDISCOVERING YOUR AUTHENTIC SELF

Your inner child is your most authentic self. It represents spontaneity, curiosity, and freedom from social expectations. It allows you to explore the world with wonder and embrace your true passions and interests without fear of judgment.

The roles of adulthood often force people to suppress these childlike qualities in favor of appearing mature and responsible. They devalue play and discourage wonder. When people spend much of their time performing adult roles, they tend to forget the role that play served earlier in life. They lose touch with a core part of themselves, replacing the voice of their inner child in their mind with the voice of external expectation.

Focusing on performance makes you lose the effortless confidence and expansiveness that comes from your inner child. This confidence gets replaced with self-doubt and restrictiveness. Instead of drawing confidence from your intrinsic curiosity, joy, and resilience, you become dependent on external validation. You place too much weight on audience reactions—what other people think of you—and you lose trust in your inner self. You second-guess your actions and decisions, leading to increased anxiety and insecurity. Sound familiar?

Performing roles also suppresses authenticity and individual self-expression. Children are naturally creative because they express themselves authentically, without concern for social norms or others' judgments. To them, life isn't a performance; it's just playtime.

Suppressing your inner child stifles the creativity and instinctive self-expression you bring to moments of play. When you're unable to express yourself authentically, you may start to question your own worth and abilities, leading to a diminished sense of confidence. The less you let your inner child guide your life as an adult, the harder it is to validate your internal voice, find fulfillment, and embrace your true self.

Neglecting your inner child doesn't make you more mature or adultlike; it just makes you lose your playful, curious, and authentic nature. When you prioritize social roles and adulthood's expectations, you miss out on believing in yourself, your passions, and your dreams. You lose a vital source of inner strength and confidence.

YOUR INNER CHILD HAS UNBOUNDED CONFIDENCE

Your inner child is an innate source of self-assurance that's with you wherever you go. It's a part of you that's free from self-doubt and exudes unbounded confidence. This unbounded confidence stems from your inner child's natural curiosity, nonjudgmental perspective, and unfiltered view of the world. Unburdened by the roles of adulthood, young children approach life with an open heart and mind. They're enthusiastic and ready to explore, learn, and embrace new experiences without the weight of societal expectations or self-doubt.

Young children see the world as a place full of possibilities. They aren't yet constrained by the fears and limitations that come with internalizing social roles and suppressing their authentic instincts and desires. This unfiltered perspective allows children to take risks, make mistakes, and acquire new abilities without the fear of failure. They approach challenges with a can-do attitude and, when they do fail, they get right back up and try again. They're naturally confident in their abilities—and guided by their resilience—because they haven't been taught to doubt themselves.

Self-doubt isn't a natural instinct. It's something we learn by suppressing our inner child and performing roles of adulthood.

Seeing the world as filled with endless possibilities, children are curious about everything. They explore their surroundings with enthusiasm and a desire to understand the world around them. Much of playtime for children revolves around informative exploration. For example, children develop rhythm and express emotions by dancing to music, understand geometry by playing with blocks, and learn about how social collaboration and rules work through imaginative group play.

Their curiosity drives young children to ask questions, experiment, and discover new things without worrying about judgment from others or themselves. It's through this process of exploration that children build their knowledge, develop skills, and feel increasingly capable in their own skin, without even realizing it.

When you reconnect with your inner child, you can recapture this sense of limitless potential. Seeing the world through the eyes of a curious child can reignite your confidence by stripping away the self-imposed limitations that hold you back. By reminding yourself that failure is a natural part of the learning process and that exploration for its own sake can be rewarding, you can turn everyday events into moments of play. You become more in touch with your authentic self and bounce back more easily from adversity.

Adopting a mindset of play into your adult life can help you reconnect with the unbounded confidence of your inner child. Whether it's through pursuing hobbies, creating art, spending time in nature, or simply rethinking your daily approach at work, you can embrace a childlike mindset and express yourself with less self-doubt.

REDISCOVERING YOUR INNER CHILD

To develop a truly authentic and resilient sense of confidence, you need to rediscover the mindset of a child. That mindset is within you right now: It's your inner child. The best way to reconnect with your inner child is by incorporating play into your life in a way that feels genuine to who you are.

Play serves as a bridge between your adult self and your inner child, connecting the present you to a less inhibited version of yourself. It allows you to break free from the constraints of adult life and rediscover the simple pleasures that bring you joy and ease your self-doubts.

Start by reflecting on your purest sources of joy. Think about the activities, hobbies, passions, values, and interests you've pursued in your life simply because they bring you happiness. These can be things you do now or things you did many years ago. It might be drawing with chalk on the sidewalk as a child, volunteering at an animal shelter, or painting. It might be playing board games with friends, baking at home, or engaging in a sport. For me, two things that come to mind are playing ping pong and performing improv.

These activities are your forms of play. They should be intrinsically motivated, freely chosen, and enjoyable. Chances are, they also allow you to harness your creativity, express your individuality, and lose track of time, enabling you to relax and live in the moment.

Once you've identified a few forms of play, commit to doing them more often. Make time for play in your daily routine, even if it's just for a few minutes each day. Make play a priority in your life.

If you find it challenging to schedule time for play, then try embracing spontaneity—just as a child would. Allow moments of playfulness to naturally pop up in your daily life. Break away from your routines and do something fun and unexpected. Here are some simple ideas to get you started:

- Sing along to music while you drive.
- Take a break during the workday to doodle on a piece of paper.
- Decorate your meal creatively when cooking dinner.
- Make up a silly song while doing chores.
- Try a fun workout, like Hula-Hooping.
- Collect a few leaves while on a walk.
- Blow bubbles into the wind.
- Spend a few extra minutes playing with a pet or young child in your life.
- Instead of walking, try skipping somewhere.
- Dance in your living room.

If any of these ideas sound silly or ridiculous to you, then you're right—they *are* silly and ridiculous. That's the point! If their silliness makes them feel unappealing to you, then that's a sign you're thinking like a performative adult, caught up in the myth of maturity and worried about judgment, whether from yourself or others. Resist this instinct. It's a trap. Step into the silliness and rediscover the joy that comes from play.

Opportunities for play are all around you, and they naturally bring out your inner child. Take those opportunities up. Embrace them. And remember, play isn't just an activity; it's a mindset. It's a choice you make. You have the power to turn almost anything into a playful experience, and when you do, your inner child becomes more present in your mind.

Young children approach life with a deep sense of play because everything is new to them. Playfulness is the mind's key to learning and exploring new things effectively. To channel your inner child, encourage yourself to branch out. Try new activities or hobbies that allow you to be playful and curious. Sign up for a new class, visit a museum, or read about a subject you know little about. Try a new sport, a new card game, a new exercise class, or a new walking path. Do anything you can to override your current script and stop *performing* life so you can actually start *living* it again.

When you approach a new activity with curiosity and a desire to understand how it works, you can step into the mind of a child and play mindfully in the present moment. The sheer act of exploration keeps your mind playful, creative, and engaged.

To fully embrace moments of play, let go of perfectionism and concerns about outcomes. Play is all about the experience itself, not the result. Focusing on the outcome takes your mind out of play and suppresses your inner child, causing you to worry about success and failure. These worries are forms of self-judgment that can strip away confidence. Children cower and retreat under the weight of perfectionism, and so do adults. The only difference is that when we're grown, we're better at disguising it. Be kind to yourself just as you'd be kind to a young child—because, deep down, we all hold that child inside us.

Perfectionism silences your inner child. Play gives them back their voice.

As you quiet your need for perfectionism, your capacity for self-expression grows. Embracing imperfection and the act of exploration allows you to settle fully into moments of play. These nonjudgmental moments build up your inner child's voice, enhancing your authenticity and self-acceptance.

The more time you spend playing, the more your inner child takes control of your mind and the more confident you become. Embracing play can be a powerful way to reconnect with your true self, providing a sanctuary of peace and creativity in a busy world. Playing for the sake of pure intrinsic joy keeps you present in the moment and less attuned to the noise of the world. You're unconcerned with societal restrictions or expectations, and you step out of the roles of adulthood. As those roles fade from your mind, you become less judgmental of yourself and others, fostering a sense of calm self-assurance. By tapping into your inner child, you rekindle the freedom and unbounded confidence you experienced in your earliest years.

CONFIDENCE, DISTILLED

Play Is Essential. Play is a fundamental psychological need that fosters creativity, authenticity, and self-esteem.

Play Challenges Adult Norms. Adulthood often glorifies seriousness and responsibility and devalues play, which suppresses your inner child and fuels self-doubt.

Embrace Spontaneity. Reconnect with your inner child by incorporating spontaneity and playfulness into your daily life.

Pursue Curiosity over Perfection. Approach new activities with inquisitiveness, enjoying the process of exploration while letting go of perfectionism.

Prioritize Joy. Identify activities that bring you pure joy and make them a regular part of your routine.

Chapter 10

QUIETING YOUR SOCIAL COMPARISONS

As a kid, I loved watching professional wrestling. The showmanship, acrobatics, and the dramatic nature of grown men body-slamming one another across the ring were exhilarating. I wanted to be like the wrestlers I saw on TV: strong, fearless, and unstoppable.

To me, wrestling wasn't about fighting. It wasn't about conflict, pain, or toxic masculinity. It was about self-expression and overcoming obstacles. It depicted a world where each wrestler developed their own brand, flaunted their unique flair, and achieved physical feats that seemed impossible. In many ways, wrestling was a metaphor for what I wanted in my life.

Watching wrestling taught me a lot about the power of self-discovery in developing confidence. Each wrestler brought their own persona into the ring, complete with signature moves, outfits, and a style of trash-talking. No matter their size, strength, or age, each wrestler entered the ring with an unapologetic embrace of their character and an enthusiasm for their unique qualities. Within this theatrical production, a wrestler's individuality gave their character a sense of meaning and direction, a sense of pride and capability. It gave them confidence.

I seized the first opportunity I had to pursue wrestling myself, joining my middle school's wrestling team when I was twelve. Of course, my school wasn't putting on WWE exhibition matches; we were practicing a structured sport with strict rules. But my motivation was the same: I wanted to feel the empowerment I saw in the wrestlers on TV. I wanted to feel *able.*

As it turns out, wrestling isn't as easy as it looks on TV. My first few practices were brutal. I was the smallest guy on the team and the only one with a physical disability. I struggled to keep up during team workouts and went home sore each day, wondering why I kept coming back the next. I couldn't get my body to perform some of the foundational wrestling drills, and when I asked the coach if I could sit those drills out, he told me to keep trying or see myself out the door. *Ouch.*

I didn't fit in, and everyone else on the team knew it. At one practice, when the coach was distracted, a teammate twice my weight locked my legs and dragged me around the mat to show everyone that I was featherlight and helpless. He wasn't wrong.

I finished the season with an 0–10 record: ten matches wrestled, ten matches lost. Utterly abysmal by any objective measure, but a remarkable success in my eyes. I'd survived a whole season on a wrestling team meant for far rougher and tougher guys than I, guys who didn't have cerebral palsy. I never quit. I showed up every day and worked to get better.

I ended my wrestling season with a sense of achievement, an awareness of my resilience, and a profound boost in confidence. I felt proud of myself and felt capable of overcoming barriers. Only a few years earlier, I'd worn braces on my legs just so I could walk right and splints on my hands so they could function. I'd been in physical therapy developing basic mobility skills and in occupational therapy learning how to tie my own shoes. Yet here I was, training and competing against my able-bodied peers as though I, too, had nothing holding me back.

I wasn't ruminating over my 0–10 record, as I knew that it was simply a social comparison. My record only showed how I'd fared against other wrestlers. What truly mattered was how I'd fared against myself. The version of me who ended that season was stronger, tougher, more perseverant, and more self-assured than the one who started it. That final version of me was a testament to how far I'd come in my life and how far I could continue to go.

> **Don't compare yourself to others. Compare who you are today to who you used to be.**

Throughout the entire wrestling season, I knew where the door was—but I never let myself open it.

SELF-COMPARISON OVER SOCIAL COMPARISON

My wrestling experience taught me a valuable lesson: The most important comparison is the one you make with yourself. By quieting the noise of social comparisons and focusing on my own progress, I could build a stronger sense of confidence that stems from within.

Social comparison is a subtle psychological poison, and it's unfairly biased against you from the start. When you compare yourself to others, you judge your insides by someone else's outsides. Much of the time, you don't see their struggles, failures, or insecurities; you see only their highlight reel. This can make you feel like you're not good enough. For introverts, the sting can be especially sharp. Comparisons don't just pass through the mind; they linger, replaying in quiet moments. And because the spotlight so often rewards extroverted qualities like charisma and social dominance, introverts are left measuring themselves against traits that may not reflect their own strengths, making the game feel doubly rigged.

When you compare yourself to others, you judge your insides by someone else's outsides.

Unlike social comparison, self-comparison focuses on your own journey and growth. Instead of comparing yourself to other people, you compare your current self to your past self—who you are today compared to who you used to be. It's about recognizing where you started, acknowledging the progress you've made, and setting future goals. Where social comparison is toxic, self-comparison is empowering. It allows you to measure your success by your own standards, not by the achievements of others.

When you look back at your life, reflect on the strides you've made. Recall times when you've overcome obstacles, learned new skills, or built resilience. Recognize that growth often comes with setbacks and that these setbacks aren't failures but part of the process.

Remind yourself that everyone's path is different and what works for someone else may not be right for you. Acknowledge your efforts and give yourself credit for times when you've worked hard and persevered, regardless of whether it led you to "success." Redirect your focus away from outcomes and toward your process.

Your process is the only thing that truly matters for understanding your worth. It lets you compare yourself to yourself without concern for how others appear. Outcomes are relative and often belong to chance; process is absolute and belongs to choice. By focusing on your process, you honor your unique path and appreciate your personal growth in ways external metrics can't measure. It reinforces your individuality and places your confidence back where it belongs: in your own hands.

SOCIAL COMPARISON IS THE ENEMY OF SELF-BELIEF

When left unchecked, social comparison can be a constant source of anxiety and insecurity. Measuring your worth against other people's lives and accomplishments forces you to live behind the scenes of their highlight reel. This comparison isn't just unfair; it's also self-defeating. It teaches you to undervalue your own worth by default.

Social comparison rewrites your worth with someone else's pen.

Our minds are naturally inclined to notice differences between ourselves and others, and in a hyperconnected world, these differences are magnified. Living in the digital age, it's easy to get caught in this trap. Humans have had an instinct to compare themselves to others for millennia; it's nothing new. From an evolutionary standpoint, social comparison was advantageous: It helped our early ancestors assess social status, resources, and belonging in their communities, all of which were crucial for survival. We still make these assessments today—only now, the arenas have shifted from villages and tribes to classrooms, offices, and social feeds. Social comparison itself is ancient. The internet and social media, however, are new, and they've amplified this ancient instinct to the point where it feels inescapable.

Social media bombards us with curated highlights of other people's lives, making it seem like everyone else is happier, more successful, and more accomplished than we are. It can feel like everyone but you is living a perfect life. Seeing these idealized images and stories can make you feel inadequate, not due to any inherent flaw in yourself but because of the distorted comparisons you unconsciously engage in with these highlight reels.

Constantly defining yourself in relation to others lowers your self-esteem, magnifies your existing self-doubts, and creates new self-doubts that eat away at your confidence. Because you live solely within your own mind, you can never truly know what goes on inside the minds of others. It's impossible. You can hear their words and observe their actions, but you never fully understand their feelings from the inside out. As a result, your mind fills in the gaps, creating stories about other people's emotions and projecting your own insecurities onto them rather than reflecting any true reality. When you engage in social comparison, you emerge with biased ideas about yourself, allowing your insecurities to gain more control over your feelings.

THE THREE PLAGUES OF SOCIAL COMPARISON

Social comparison is toxic to self-confidence for three main reasons: It focuses on impossible ideals, drives loneliness, and is externally focused. Introverts may be predisposed to experience these three plagues especially acutely.

Plague #1: Impossible Ideals. The first major problem with social comparison is that it often focuses on impossible ideals. It leads your mind to focus on depictions that simply aren't realistic. Take body image, for example. While body image can be a concern for everyone, young women especially suffer from comparing their bodies to those they see in movies, magazines, and social media. The ideals shown in the media are often unattainable distortions of reality—frequently enhanced through image-editing software—and feature a select group of people. Yet, they make perfectly healthy individuals feel as though something is wrong with their bodies. And body image is just one example. These distorted comparisons show up in every arena of life—from careers to relationships to lifestyles—creating unrealistic standards across the board. Social comparison shifts your reference point to an impossible ideal, making you feel inadequate no matter what you do. There's no winning.

> **Social comparison shows a trailer, never the full movie.**

Plague #2: Loneliness. A second problem is loneliness. When people use social media, they often emerge feeling more isolated than they did a few minutes prior, precisely because of social comparison. The irony is that social media is intended to create social *connection,* not isolation. Viewing the curated social lives of others can make you feel inadequate and insecure about your own friendships and relationships. These self-evaluations stem purely from the outer focus of social comparison. They're ways in which your mind questions your self-esteem by redefining your own success (or lack thereof) based on idealized images that show the most positive aspects of others' lives, not their reality.

Plague #3: External Focus. A third problem with social comparison is its external focus. When you form ideas about yourself based on what you observe in others, you train your mind to seek contentment externally. This means placing your self-esteem in the hands of societal trends, norms, and the majority's opinions. As a result, you lose touch with your inner sense of self and your personal values. Instead of being guided by your inner voice and goals, you become influenced by what seems popular or acceptable to others. This shift in focus leads to a constant chase for validation and approval, making your self-worth fragile and dependent on external factors. Ultimately, you sacrifice your ability to be the true judge of your own life, undermining your inner peace and your authentic belief in who you are.

HOW TO STOP YOUR SOCIAL COMPARISONS

Social comparison is an instinct deeply ingrained in the human mind. From a young age, we learn to gauge our worth and abilities by comparing ourselves to others. However, the more we do this, the less we feel our worth from within and the less confidence we have in ourselves.

If you find yourself engaging in social comparisons often, it's important to find ways to nip these comparisons in the bud. Being able to control your social comparisons—and ultimately stop them altogether—is crucial for developing confidence. It allows you to rediscover your authentic self and build self-acceptance. Here are some ways you can regain control over your mind by quieting social comparisons and replacing them with healthier alternatives.

Monitor Your Social Media Use

Be aware of how much time you spend on social media. Ideally, limit it as much as you can while still maintaining the meaningful social connections you value in your life. Use social media more mindfully and intentionally, avoiding endless scrolling at all costs.

Start by setting boundaries around your social media use. Designate specific times of the day for using social media or set time limits on how much you allow yourself to use it each day. Use your phone's settings to set exact time limits on your apps—and, yes, actually stick to them. Some other boundaries you can try include leaving your phone in another room during meals, turning it off an hour before bed, or waiting an hour upon waking up before using it. These small resets give your mind a break and help you notice how often you reach for your phone out of habit, without even realizing it.

To take things a step further, consider taking a social media detox where you stay off these platforms altogether. A detox may be as short or as long as you want. For some people, it means going a few hours without your phone nearby. For other people, it's deleting all social media apps for a whole month. Start small, and know that any amount of time away from social media can help you become more mindful and in control of your usage.

When you do use social media, curate your feeds to support your well-being. Not all social media use is the same. There are so many wonderful creators on social media who share motivational, educational, and uplifting content. But there are also corners of these platforms that suck you into mindless doomscrolls and "look how good my life is" posts. Pay attention to which accounts trigger negative social comparisons in your mind and make you question yourself or feel inadequate. Unfollow or mute those accounts and avoid similar content.

Remember, you have control over what you see and engage with online. Your mind is what you fill it with.

Cultivate Awareness

Self-awareness is power. Becoming aware of your own mind sounds simple, yet most people neglect to do it. Often, we slip into comparing ourselves to others without even realizing it, subconsciously letting these thoughts infiltrate our minds and chip away at our self-esteem. Not realizing that social comparison is happening, we wonder why we feel so lonely, inadequate, and anxious.

Cultivating awareness is crucial for freeing yourself from the cycle of social comparison. Awareness means recognizing moments of social comparison while they're happening and making a conscious effort to redirect your thoughts away from them. By becoming mindful of when and why you compare yourself to others, you can take proactive steps to stop these comparisons in their tracks and prevent them from turning into self-doubt.

The first step in developing this awareness is to tune in to your emotional responses throughout the day. Feelings of envy, inadequacy, or self-doubt are like flashing red lights, signaling that you're engaging in social comparison. For example, if you feel a sudden pang of jealousy when you see a friend's vacation photos or hear about a colleague's promotion, take a moment to pause and reflect. Ask yourself, "Am I comparing my life to theirs?" By recognizing these feelings, you can label them as irrelevant to your true self and give them less weight, preventing them from spiraling into deeper dissatisfaction.

This process of cultivating awareness isn't about suppressing your emotions or criticizing yourself for how you feel. It's about acknowledging these feelings with compassion and understanding. Recognize that it's human to compare, but remind yourself that everyone's journey is different. Your path is uniquely yours, and it's okay to have moments of self-doubt. The key is to catch these moments and see them for what they are: biased effects of social comparison, not truths about yourself. Give less weight to these thoughts by understanding that they don't accurately reflect your worth—and, in fact, that they have nothing to do with you at all.

Shift Your Focus Inward

One of the most effective ways to combat social comparison in the long term is to maintain your focus on yourself—not on other people. Instead of preoccupying yourself with what everyone else is up to, concentrate on your own journey, progress, and achievements.

Measuring your worth against others is a recipe for disaster. It's on outward focus that leaves you feeling chronically uneasy, jumping between emotional highs and lows. Cultivating an inward focus, meanwhile, allows you to feel more emotionally stable. It grants you more compassion for yourself and promotes enduring resilience. It allows you to appreciate your unique strengths and experiences.

You can begin this shift inward by practicing gratitude. Reflecting on the positive aspects of your life regularly cultivates a sense of contentment that is unwavering in the face of social comparisons. One strategy is to start a gratitude journal, writing down a few things you're thankful for each day. Research shows that this simple exercise can transform your mindset, training your mind to focus on the positive qualities you have rather than those you feel you lack. More broadly, journaling of any kind helps. Putting thoughts on paper gives them shape, calms the mind, and reveals patterns you might miss if they only stay in your head. Another benefit? Journaling lets you track your progress over time, allowing you to compare your present self to your past self; it encourages self-comparison in place of social comparison.

Another way to shift your focus inward is by setting personal goals. These goals should be specific, realistic, and aligned with things you truly value and enjoy. When people pursue clear goals that they've defined for themselves, they feel a greater sense of purpose and are less swayed by what others are doing. Their own progress—rather than how they stack up against others—becomes their measure of success.

Focusing on personal growth and self-improvement helps reprogram your focus away from social comparisons. Engage in activities that bring you joy, immerse you in flow, help you learn new skills, and contribute to your overall sense of fulfillment.

As you pursue personal growth, take time to recognize and celebrate your achievements. Appreciating yourself builds self-esteem and reduces the urge to compare yourself to others. Reflect on your accomplishments, no matter how small they may seem. Celebrate your progress and milestones, reminding yourself of the hard work and effort that went into achieving them. By focusing on your efforts, you can reinforce your resilience and cultivate a sense of pride in your unique journey that can't be compared to others.

FEWER COMPARISONS, MORE CONFIDENCE

Building confidence doesn't happen overnight; it's an ongoing journey. Shifting your urge to seek validation externally toward finding self-assurance within takes time and happens incrementally, in small steps, rather than a sudden sea change. Each step you take that is guided by your own internal compass of self-acceptance makes your mind feel calmer and more grounded, less derailed by factors beyond your control.

Everyone has their own battles and triumphs, making social comparisons ultimately meaningless. Your path is unique and incomparable. It grants you your individuality, and no comparison should take that away from you.

True confidence blooms when you realize that you're valuable simply for being yourself, not for what you've accomplished or how you measure up to others. Self-worth isn't something you need to earn; it's a given. You just need to rediscover it. Quieting your social comparisons allows you to do just that, giving this psychological gift to yourself instead of searching for it in the outer world.

You're valuable simply for being yourself, not for what you've accomplished or how you measure up to others.

Living with cerebral palsy has hindered my life in countless ways, causing physical pain, mental frustration, and logistical obstacles. I still can barely tie my own shoes, for crying out loud. . . . Yet, in many ways, I deeply value my experience having cerebral palsy. It's made me who I am. Knowing nothing other than my own experience in life, I know firsthand no deficit, no lacking, no discontentment. The only deficits I know come from times when I compare myself to others. Those comparisons don't serve me; they just pull me away from my true self.

CONFIDENCE, DISTILLED

Social Comparison Is Distorted. Social comparison leads you to judge your insides by someone else's outsides, creating a skewed assessment of your own worth.

Cultivate Awareness. Be mindful of when you're engaging in social comparison and consciously redirect your thoughts toward self-acceptance. Limit your social media use to avoid unnecessary comparisons.

Embrace Self-Comparison. Choose self-comparison over social comparison. Focus on comparing your current self to your past self, acknowledging your personal growth and your progress.

Value Your Individuality. Understand that everyone's journey is unique. Value yourself for who you are, not how you measure up to others.

Chapter 11

EMBRACING HUMOR

My whole life, I've had one of those disability parking placards—first when my parents drove me around as a kid and later when I got my own license. In Los Angeles, a disability placard does more than just let you park in reserved disability spots; it also allows you to park in dozens of other restricted zones and even lets you skip on paying for parking meters. Just park your car in any metered spot, put up your placard, and be on your way. It's my favorite perk of being disabled (and it's also the most budget-friendly).

But I have a complicated relationship with my disability placard. On one hand, it lets me park anywhere and saves me hundreds of dollars a year. On the other hand, it's an inescapably public signal to the world that I'm disabled.

While I take pride in being a person with a disability, disclosing my disability is an act of vulnerability I want control over. Stigma is real, and people carry stereotypes and misunderstandings about differences. I want to disclose my disability with intention, when and how I feel most comfortable. I don't want a parking placard to do it for me.

Plus, cerebral palsy can be complicated. Many people haven't heard of it, and even those who are familiar with it need some clarity as there are so many different types of cerebral palsy with their own symptoms and limitations. When I tell someone new in my life that I have cerebral palsy, I want at least a few minutes to explain what that really means for me.

The trickiest area of my life with this is dating. I have a three-date rule (no, not that kind of three-date rule . . .). Generally, I don't bring up my cerebral palsy until the third date. By that point, it feels like the right time to broach this vulnerable self-disclosure, get to know each other more deeply, and see if we can truly understand, accept, and support each other.

When I go on first or second dates, I bite the bullet and pay for metered parking. I hide my disability placard away so there's no chance my date can see it. This way, I get to enjoy the date without having to explain the rawest parts of my life story to a stranger; that is, until I forget to bring quarters for the meter and desperately need free parking. . . .

One evening when I was in my mid-twenties, I found myself quarterless and unable to pay for a meter when parking for a first date, so I caved and put up my disability placard. I ended up giving my date a ride home afterward, completely forgetting that my placard was up—loud and proud. As my date got into my car, she exclaimed, "Whoa! You have a disability placard? You are so lucky!"

I was mortified.

All I heard were her first few words: acknowledging that I have a disability parking placard. As I mentally prepared myself for an impromptu explanation of cerebral palsy, I reheard her last few words: that I'm . . . lucky?

Now, I was just perplexed. I was also skeptical of this woman's understanding of why people obtain disability placards in the first place.

I didn't know it at the time, but I'd just received comedic gold. Shortly after this date, I performed a stand-up comedy set titled "Cerebral Palsy Is an Aphrodisiac." That set ultimately inspired the one I improvised to win my national comedy championship.

COMEDY AGAINST ALL ODDS

Earlier in my life, I never imagined doing stand-up comedy—because earlier in my life, I could barely stand up (get it?). Pursuing any kind of performance onstage just wasn't a path I'd considered. I'm an introvert. My body looks and moves awkwardly. And I'm an academic. I write papers with words like "thus" and "theorize" in them, not comedy sets.

While I always flaunted a sense of humor with friends, I never saw myself onstage making an audience laugh. That was until I saw a comedy show by Drew Lynch.

Drew is a professional comedian who gained recognition when he finished in second place on *America's Got Talent* in 2015. Earlier in his life, Drew developed a debilitating stutter due to a sports injury, and that stutter is now the foundation of his career. When I saw Drew perform live, he spoke about his experiences living with his stutter, using humor to find joy and strength in his struggles and to raise awareness about disability. He was relatable, inspirational, and incredibly self-confident in front of all these strangers in the audience.

Watching Drew perform, I felt a sudden urge to turn my experiences with cerebral palsy into comedic bits. I wanted to find humor in my own struggles, inspiring and entertaining audiences in the process.

Shortly after I saw Drew perform, a friend introduced me to a local comedy coach, Corey Martin Craig. Corey shared his perspective with me: The best comedy comes from overcoming adversity, embracing your unique authenticity, and being vulnerable with your audience. Corey taught me that "the funny" in comedy isn't outside you; it's within you. Of course, this spoke to my soul.

When I told Corey I have cerebral palsy, we clicked. The next day, he became my comedy coach, cast me in an upcoming show he was producing, and my comedy journey took off from there.

Since meeting Corey, I've performed dozens of shows at venues around Los Angeles, in front of audiences as small as ten and as large as five hundred. I've connected with all kinds of people through my performances, meeting people from walks of life I would have never met otherwise. The irony was that I would disclose the deepest struggles of life with cerebral palsy to masses of strangers with ease while still maintaining my three-date rule in my personal life.

Humor grants you permission to be yourself; it turns vulnerability into levity, and self-doubt into self-love.

From this, I realized that humor grants permission. Humor grants your mind permission to engage with and process difficult thoughts, feelings, and pains. It grants other people permission to hear your most vulnerable stories with comfort, in a way that feels connected enough to create empathy and understanding, yet distant enough to maintain lightness and prevent overstepping. Humor is its own kind of vulnerability equilibrium. The beauty of comedy lies within this safe zone of human connection, and that connection only happens when a comedian first connects with themself.

Humor granted me permission to simply be—to express myself authentically, with less self-doubt—and comedy became an outlet where I could see light where darkness lives. Take my hands, for example. My hand muscles are so uncoordinated and spastic that even though I'm twenty-nine years old, I still can't cut my own toenails without risking a trip to the emergency room. When most people go on a first date, they wonder if they're about to fall for this person emotionally. When I go on a date, I worry if I'll fall for my date physically, as I might trip over my own feet while walking over to say hello.

To process the tougher feelings within your mind and quiet down the self-doubts they create, it's important to embrace humor. Laugh at life and at yourself. The more you strip down your walls with a lighter outlook, the more you discover who you truly are in a compassionate and accepting way. Often, finding humor where pain lives has the power to heal, connect, and liberate you from the barriers of your own mind. Finding humor in these situations can provide a release and a way to reframe challenges positively.

A FUNNY LIFE IS A CONFIDENT LIFE

Having a sense of humor in your life doesn't mean you need to be a polished comedian. It doesn't mean you know how to tell jokes, work a crowd, or even be funny at all. A sense of humor isn't a skill; it's a mindset.

A sense of humor isn't a skill. It's a mindset.

Most people take themselves and their lives too seriously. They get so caught up in performing their adult roles—clinging tightly to their identities, political affiliations, and life goals—that they forget how to let their guard down and joke for the sake of joking. Laughter is medicine—for yourself and for those around you. Few people laugh as much as they should, and their mental health, happiness, and confidence suffer as a result.

When you live life with a sense of humor, you choose to see the funny wherever you go. You see the world as full of ironies, coincidences, and hidden delights. You choose to laugh at the absurdities of life rather than letting them bring you down.

Having a sense of humor is a choice, and embracing humor means making your default response to life events more lighthearted. It's being able to laugh at yourself and choosing not to take yourself too seriously. By supporting your vulnerability, promoting self-acceptance, and building resilience, developing your sense of humor can go a long way toward boosting your confidence.

Having a sense of humor helps quiet self-doubts that stem from a negative inner dialogue. When you take yourself too seriously, it's easy to be overly critical of yourself as negative self-talk fills your mind. Lightening up and finding the funny in life changes the tone of this inner dialogue, replacing self-criticism with self-acceptance. It makes you like yourself more.

Humor silences self-doubt. When you laugh at yourself, you turn self-criticism into self-acceptance.

By laughing at your mistakes and slipups, you're letting yourself know that it's okay to be imperfect and that, in fact, your imperfections are what make you human. Practicing the art of laughing at yourself builds the kind of self-compassion that underlies the ability to be confident. It trains your mind to accept who you are.

Any time you find yourself criticizing yourself for something you've done, take a moment to remove yourself from your own shoes. Imagine what you'd think if, instead of having done that thing yourself, you watched a character in a comedic television show do it. Reimagine how trivial and even entertaining your behavior would be if it took place in that kind of fictional world for others to enjoy watching it. Make those small missteps less personal. Find the funny in them.

Odds are, you do funny, absurd things all the time. You're just too caught up in your ego, narrative, and adulthood roles to see it (yes, that's a callback to Chapters 6 and 9). If you're like most people, you've sent a text to the wrong group chat, waved back at someone who wasn't waving at you, tripped over nothing on the sidewalk, or spilled coffee on yourself before a big meeting. These little blunders happen all the time, yet instead of laughing at them, our default reaction is embarrassment, frustration, or self-criticism. We convince ourselves that these slipups are reflections of our competence or worth when really they're just the comic relief of being human.

The problem with these moments isn't that we mess up; it's that we take those moments too seriously. When you take yourself too seriously, your mind blows every mistake you make or every weakness you have out of proportion. Whether it's making a conversational blunder at a social gathering or messing up a task at work, failure can feel like a heavy threat to your self-worth. But when you take a step back from your own life, view yourself from the perspective of an observer, and laugh at yourself, you can stop your mind from overanalyzing your flaws. When you drown out your ego, step outside the story you're telling yourself, and see the humor in the chaos, you'll realize how often you—and other people in your life—create accidental comedy. Choosing to laugh at it doesn't just lighten your mood; it turns threats to your self-image into proof that you're imperfect, relatable, and resilient.

Humor lives in the moment. In moments of humor, nothing is personal; it's just observational. Because humor is all about interpreting events in your life with lightness and satire, it trains your mind to observe and process rather than to ruminate and stagnate. When you find humor in your struggles, you can more easily process difficult parts of your life and understand them from a variety of angles without feeling like they're a personal threat. You can see failure as a single instance to reflect on, reinterpret, and grow from—not as a definitive judgment of your abilities.

The power of humor to separate your actions, life events, and struggles from your sense of self makes it easier to maintain confidence in hard times. When you laugh at yourself, you feel lighter. You don't worry about mistakes or failure as much. You don't ruminate over the worst case that might happen in the future or the "what ifs" of the past. When you search for humor in your mistakes, those experiences become less intimidating. They carry less weight in your mind and seem more manageable.

There's a reason why self-deprecating humor is so popular among successful comedians. Laughing at yourself shows that you're comfortable with your imperfections and that you aren't afraid to be vulnerable. It's a sign of self-confidence. And people gravitate toward that energy.

HUMOR PRIMES YOUR MIND FOR CONFIDENCE

Embracing your flaws with humor shows healthy vulnerability, self-acceptance, and adaptive resilience. The irony is that laughing at yourself doesn't bring you down; it lifts you up. When you can laugh at your own shortcomings, you show others—and yourself—that you're secure in who you are, which in turn boosts your sense of self-worth.

Lightening up lets you live more authentically, allowing you to be true to yourself with less fear of judgment. Because laughing at yourself often involves leaning into your quirks and idiosyncrasies, embracing humor helps you feel more comfortable in your skin. This is precisely what I've done in my comedy career: reframing my cerebral palsy as an ironically positive and entertaining part of my life.

Just as humor builds up your self-acceptance by allowing you to be vulnerable in healthy, comfortable ways, it also promotes resilience by regulating your stress and anxiety. Feeling anxious is a major barrier to confidence because anxiety triggers self-doubt and negative thinking. Anxiety pushes your mind to focus on all possible negative outcomes while ignoring positive opportunities. It prevents you from believing in your abilities, putting you in a constant state of worry, fear, hesitation, and avoidance.

If humor were a medicinal pill, it'd be one of the most prescribed treatments for anxiety. Humor is an incredibly effective stress-reliever. When you laugh, your brain releases endorphins, which are neurotransmitters that make you feel good. They're your body's natural painkillers. They're why laughing feels so good.

If humor were a medicinal pill, it'd be one of the most prescribed treatments for anxiety.

Through these endorphins, laughter immediately melts away feelings of stress and anxiety. Laughter also involves deep breathing, helping you get more oxygen into your lungs and stimulating circulation, which can relax your muscles and alleviate physical tension. Additionally, laughter quiets down your sympathetic nervous system, allowing your heart rate and blood pressure to decrease to normal levels when they rise due to stress—just like meditation does. These physiological effects have powerful psychological impacts, making you feel even more relaxed and in control of your mind.

By applying your sense of humor and allowing yourself to laugh during times of stress, you can clear your mind and calm yourself down when you need it most. You become more in touch with your inner child and boost your resilience as you become better able to handle challenging situations. This resilience lets you remain confident in a wider variety of situations, enabling you to think clearly, act decisively, and maintain a positive outlook in the face of stress.

The more you choose to have a sense of humor in your life, the more your mind will embrace humor over time. You'll train yourself to have a richer sense of humor, and naturally, looking at life on the lighter side will become your mind's default. This shift in mindset will let you feel more authentic and comfortable laughing at your true self. That lightness will, in turn, make you feel less weighed down by self-doubt and more authentically confident.

HUMOR LENDS A FEELING OF CONTROL

A big reason why humor helps you develop confidence is that it makes you feel more in control of your life. Humans have a fundamental need to feel like they're in the driver's seat. We live in an uncertain world full of randomness, and that's inherently scary. We crave a sense of control because it provides the stability, security, and predictability we so desperately want to experience.

Perhaps the best example of how essential a sense of control is to our psychological well-being is the Covid-19 pandemic. The worst times of the pandemic were unsettling for many reasons, one of which was the loss of control over our lives. We were required to stay at home, give up many of our hobbies, give up our jobs in many instances, and limit our social interactions. We were unable to plan for the future and couldn't even imagine what society might look like next month, let alone next year. The pandemic brought about a feeling of helplessness, stripping away a sense of control we didn't even realize we had until it was gone.

A sense of control allows people to navigate challenges, make decisions, and pursue their goals. When you feel in control, you're naturally more confident because you believe you can determine your future. You feel capable of harnessing your abilities, defining your own goals, and responding to challenges with resilience.

Control is like a psychological bank account: a source of mental savings you can draw upon for strength. A sense of control makes you feel protected from whatever life throws at you, allowing you to define and interpret events in your life with more choice and autonomy. It helps you predict and make sense of the world around you in a way that feels favorable.

When you live life with a sense of humor, you can reinterpret events in your life in a more lighthearted and less threatening way. This act of reinterpretation—this change of perspective—lends you a feeling of control, for while you can't always choose what happens to you in life, you do get to choose how you *define* what happens.

A sense of humor lets you separate your *experiences* from your *reactions* to those experiences. This distinction is critical because it's in your reactions that self-doubt forms and confidence dwindles. Life is what you interpret it to be. When you choose to laugh at a situation, you take an active role in shaping your interpretation and, therefore, your emotional response. You teach your mind that there can be silver linings in moments of struggle.

The act of reinterpretation through humor trains your cognitive flexibility, which is your mind's ability to shift its thinking patterns and adapt to changing events. When you come up with funny twists on situations, you force your mind to think creatively. Serious thinking is linear; funny thinking is nonlinear. Funny thinking is all over the place, and that feels liberating. It makes your mind less restricted, which is essential for harnessing confidence. Confidence is an expansive feeling that lets you explore and embrace the world around you. Because humor involves assigning multiple explanations to life events, it conditions your mind to stay flexible, expansive, and in turn confident.

Developing this cognitive flexibility over time makes you a better problem solver for anything you encounter in life. It makes you more adaptable as you start to see multiple interpretations of events and, therefore, multiple possible ways to respond to those events. By regularly exercising your sense of humor, you make your brain more agile, reducing your tendency to doubt yourself. This ability to think creatively and openly gives you a greater sense of control, allowing you to decide how you respond to what life throws your way. It helps you feel more competent and confident when facing new challenges.

DEVELOPING YOUR SENSE OF HUMOR

Embracing your sense of humor in everyday life makes it easier to feel confident. It helps you feel calmer, happier, and more capable of handling any challenges you encounter. Here are some ways to develop your sense of humor to support your confidence.

Reject the Myth of Maturity

The pressure to appear mature makes people deny their playful, silly, and childlike side. This side of you—your inner child, as discussed earlier—is a crucial part of self-expression that is normal and healthy. When you're in touch with your inner child, you approach life with a pure sense of joy and laugh often, even at the most ridiculous things. Your sense of humor is alive, prominent, and unbound.

Many people glorify maturity, viewing anything childlike as unfitting for adults. They believe that to be seen as mature, they must be serious, composed, professional, and restrained. This myth of maturity discourages adults from expressing their inner sense of humor, which is free from the roles and expectations of adulthood. When you suppress any and all instincts that seem immature, you suppress most of your true sense of humor. You start overthinking, doubting your instincts, and missing opportunities for lightheartedness.

To develop your sense of humor, it's crucial to reject the myth of maturity. Allow yourself to act and think like a child, forgetting about the expectations people have about how an adult ought to act.

Embrace spontaneity, be curious, and let yourself be silly without fear of judgment—from yourself or others. Find joy in simple pleasures, make funny faces, and laugh out loud at the silliest things. Find moments of immaturity.

Embrace Your Imperfections

Being able to laugh at yourself is a foundational element of confidence. Instead of viewing your flaws, struggles, and mistakes as failures, see them as opportunities for humor. When you take yourself less seriously, you open the door to finding humor in your shortcomings, making them seem less threatening.

Confidence isn't the absence of flaws. It's the ability to laugh at them.

Embracing your imperfections brings self-acceptance, making you more relaxed and approachable, which boosts your confidence wherever you go. When you learn to laugh at your quirks and idiosyncrasies, you naturally feel less self-conscious and social situations feel more comfortable. Sharing honest stories of your mistakes and embarrassing moments can be surprisingly funny, helping you develop your sense of humor while building rapport with others easily.

Of course, there's a line between healthy self-deprecating humor and toxic self-criticism. The difference is whether you're tearing yourself down or lightening yourself up—whether you're laughing *with* yourself or at your own expense. When you share your imperfections and celebrate your quirks in a way that uplifts you, you show others and yourself that you're not afraid to be vulnerable. This honesty and self-acceptance make others feel more comfortable around you. It also makes you feel more comfortable in your own skin by lessening the weight your imperfections have over your mind.

Be Open to Laughter

It's so simple but worth stating: Let yourself laugh freely and frequently. Sometimes, people hold back their desire to laugh because they worry it might be inappropriate or because they're self-conscious about how they sound. Let go of these inhibitions and enjoy the natural release that laughter provides. Laughter not only feels good but also strengthens your sense of humor and makes you more receptive to finding the funny all over again. Plus, it's contagious and builds connection.

Acting on your instinct to laugh is a form of self-acceptance and validation that supports your confidence. It lets you know that your authentic instincts are valid and worthy. It trains your mind to doubt itself less.

Each time you laugh without holding back, you train your mind to doubt itself less.

Take up opportunities to be playful. Look for ways to lighten your mood and laugh more, whether it's playing with pets or kids, playing sports, or playing board games with friends. These forms of play remind you not to take life too seriously and encourage you to find fun in everyday moments. Being playful encourages a mindset of wonder and openness, essential for maintaining a sense of humor.

Study Humor

While humor is a mindset, it's also an art form. That means it's something you can study and understand better. By understanding the art of humor, you train your mind to look for and recognize opportunities for a good laugh.

One way to study humor is simply to observe and notice. Humor is all around you; you just need to take the time to notice it. Work on paying attention to things in your environment as you go about your day. It could be noticing a unique sign on the road, overhearing a funny conversation at a coffee shop, or watching two dogs play at a park. The more mindful you are of these moments, the more you'll recognize and appreciate humor in everyday life. Over time, this practice can help you develop a more lighthearted outlook on life and make your sense of humor a more prominent part of your mind.

Another way to study humor is to consume it. Watch stand-up comedy shows, improv shows, and comedic movies and television. Follow social media accounts that share funny content. Read satire, humorous books, and funny stories online. Don't just consume comedy mindlessly; experience it mindfully. Notice not only that it's funny, but *why* it's funny and what about it makes you laugh. Exposing yourself to different forms of humor and observing their qualities will teach you a richer spectrum of humor styles, encouraging your mind to find and create more opportunities for humor in your own life.

Meditate

A lot of people see meditation as dull and stoic, so it may seem counterintuitive to think of meditation as a way to develop your sense of humor. But without a doubt, meditation does just that.

Practicing meditation can bring out your natural sense of humor by making you more mindful and self-aware. Meditation trains your mind to observe your own thoughts and emotions without judgment, helping you let go of self-critical thoughts that block your ability to find humor in everyday situations. By becoming more aware of the present moment and quieting your ego, you can see the absurdities and ironies of life more clearly and laugh at them more easily. Because it brings out your inner child and keeps you in the present moment, meditation prevents you from taking life too seriously. It helps you lighten up.

A particular form of meditation called loving-kindness meditation can be especially potent at enhancing your sense of humor. Loving-kindness meditation involves focusing on sending feelings of love and kindness to yourself and others. To practice it, sit quietly, close your eyes, and silently repeat phrases like "May I be happy, peaceful, safe, and at ease," gradually extending these wishes to others in your life. I know it can feel a bit woo-woo and quirky, but just try it. By making you feel more positive and connected to others, loving-kindness meditation can allow you to approach yourself and others with compassion, making it easier to laugh at your own mistakes and imperfections. In essence, it removes many of the insecurities and self-doubts that get in the way of finding humor.

From my experience with the meditation community, I've learned that the people most in touch with their sense of humor are those with the deepest meditation practice. They approach life with a lightheartedness and joy that comes from inner calm and self-acceptance. Because they're not weighed down by self-doubt or negativity, they feel free to laugh at themselves and the world around them. They don't take anything in life too seriously, so they find humor in life's imperfections. This mindset makes them confident and enjoyable to be around.

Meditation supports you in achieving each of the other strategies for activating your sense of humor: It helps you reject the myth of maturity, embrace your imperfections, appreciate the presence of humor, and take up opportunities to laugh. And these benefits are on top of the other perks of meditation for promoting a confident mind.

If you're looking to boost your confidence by developing your sense of humor, incorporating meditation into your routine might be an unexpected game-changer.

CONFIDENCE, DISTILLED

Laughter Reduces Stress and Anxiety. Laughter releases endorphins, the feel-good hormones, enhancing your resilience to life's challenges.

Humor Reframes Negative Experiences. A sense of humor allows you to reframe negative experiences, making them feel less threatening and more manageable. It empowers you to rewrite your narrative with a greater sense of control.

Humor Promotes Self-Acceptance and Authenticity. Embracing humor allows you to feel more authentic, comfortable, and confident in your own skin.

Find the Funny. Laugh at yourself, find humor in your imperfections, and avoid taking yourself too seriously. Seek out the funny moments in everyday life.

Chapter 12

A TOKEN OF CONFIDENCE

I have a guitar that rests in my living room. It has a permanent home right by my couch and just a few feet from my desk. I walk by it to get to my bedroom, can see it on my way to the bathroom, and move it aside each time I vacuum. But here's the thing: I only play it once a year.

When I was eight years old, I wanted to take up a musical instrument. I was drawn to the guitar—its aesthetic, its sound, and how cool I thought I'd look while playing it. I didn't understand how guitars worked. It seemed like you just stroke some chords with one hand and hold the guitar up with the other. And then, I figured, the magic just happens.

Unfortunately, cerebral palsy and guitar mix like oil and water. I quickly learned that playing guitar is the ultimate fine-motor workout, and you need to move your fingers around elegantly to create any pattern of sound. Unfortunately, my brain is damaged in a way that I can't control any of my fingers individually. My hands open, close, and flop around, with my fingers moving together as a single unit with no individual control. I was devastated when I realized that I wasn't able to play guitar—or piano, violin, flute, or any other popular instrument that all my classmates were starting to play.

My options were limited. I needed an instrument that bypassed the need for finger dexterity, one that would allow me to create sounds through larger motions using my arms, wrists, or legs. That's what led me to the drums. The drums suited my spastic body, and though they weren't my first choice, they were fun to play, and I stuck with them for five years.

Fast-forward to my early twenties. One afternoon, on a whim, I went out and bought a guitar. At the time, I was transitioning from college into the real world, reflecting on who I was and the person I wanted to become. I wanted to be someone who defined for myself what I could and couldn't do. And I wanted to remember that every day.

I taught myself a few basic guitar chords, spending hours figuring out how to play them in a way that worked for my body. I settled into an unconventional way of "holding" my guitar by letting it rest on my lap as I sat. I flipped it around to play left-handed, even though I'm right-handed, so I could use my dominant hand to form chords. I watched countless tutorial videos and figured out how to use my thumb and other fingers' knuckles in peculiar ways to re-create traditional chord patterns without the need to maneuver my fingers individually. Adaptation by adaptation, I made it work.

Since learning how to play these basic chords, I've barely touched my guitar. I got what I wanted from it: proof that I could defy limitations and redefine what my body was capable of. I put into practice the kind of person I wanted to be. I rewrote the rules for myself.

KEEPING A TOKEN OF CONFIDENCE

Growing up, I viewed the guitar as the epitome of what cerebral palsy prevented me from doing. By learning to play it, I rewrote my own narrative of what I was capable of. My guitar became my token of confidence—a symbol that I'm capable of pursuing any goal I set my mind to. That's why I've kept it around for all these years, resting openly in my living room. Having a personal token like this can serve as a constant quiet reminder of your capabilities and achievements, providing a source of strength and encouragement.

I believe everyone should have at least one "token of confidence." That's the term I made up for it. And here's what it means:

A token of confidence is an object that symbolizes your achievements, overcoming obstacles, and personal growth. It's a reminder of your capabilities, determination, and ability to redefine what is possible for yourself, no matter what challenges you face. It's a tangible source of inspiration you can view at any time, especially during times of doubt or difficulty.

Keep at least one token of confidence—an object that reminds you of an achievement or obstacle you've overcome.

For example, some artists hold on to a sketchbook from their early days of drawing. This sketchbook reminds them of their journey and progress, serving as a source of inspiration. On days when the artist feels stuck or doubts their talent, flipping through the pages of their early sketchbook can remind them of how far they've come. It connects who they once were to who they are now, validating their growth and dedication to their craft.

Tokens of confidence aren't just memorabilia. They don't need to have aesthetic or monetary value, nor do they need to remind you of any particular event or person. Rather, they just need to embody a significant milestone and the essence of perseverance. They're symbols of ability.

A SYMBOL OF ABILITY

There's a rich psychology behind the power of symbols. Throughout human history, symbols have played a critical role in the development of culture, communication, and personal identity. Symbols turn complex ideas, emotions, and experiences into tangible forms, allowing us to express and share aspects of our inner lives in a visual way that's easily understandable. From national flags and company logos to university diplomas and wedding rings, symbols are all around us. They help us make sense of the world and our place within it, giving our lives direction and meaning. For introverts, whose default is to process life experiences internally, symbols can provide a powerful way to validate and externalize your inner journey.

The process of symbolization involves imbuing an object with personal or social meaning. This can happen consciously or unconsciously, intentionally or unintentionally. For example, a runner might keep the shoes they wore in their first marathon at home as a token of confidence, symbolizing the progress they've made. These shoes become more than just footwear; they represent dedication, perseverance, and the realization of a goal.

A token of confidence is a specific kind of symbol that represents your inner qualities that fuel your confidence: your belief in yourself, your ambition, your resilience, and so much more. These tokens act as anchors, grounding you in your past achievements while propelling you toward new goals with an empowered mindset of self-discovery and growth. When you face new challenges, your tokens of confidence serve as proof that you've overcome obstacles before and can do so again. They build a bridge between your past successes and future pursuits, reinforcing your belief that you're capable of achieving your goals.

Symbols resonate deeply within our psyche because they operate on multiple levels of meaning. They evoke emotions, trigger memories, and validate and expand our sense of self. This is precisely why symbols can be powerful sources of motivation and self-belief: In times of self-doubt, they can remind you of experiences when you've believed in yourself and accomplished more than you thought possible.

Self-doubt often results from interpreting previous failures in your life as your own fault—as though you're personally responsible for the outcome—and as if any single mistake or failure defines your abilities. When you attach that kind of meaning to a memory, it takes on a heavy emotional weight and can make you feel inadequate. As a result, past memories can make you question your abilities and self-worth, and each time you replay a memory, the negativity compounds. Over time, the accumulation of these memories can chip away at your confidence and make you hesitant to take on new challenges.

For example, you might have had bad experiences with public speaking in school. Perhaps you stumbled over your words, noticed your audience disengaged, and felt you didn't get your points across clearly. You might then interpret this as evidence that you're terrible at public speaking, believing you'll always perform poorly in future speeches and presentations. The idea of delivering a speech again can activate this past memory, causing insecurity and anxiety in the present moment. These emotions can lead you to avoid all kinds of public speaking, ultimately limiting your opportunities for potential professional advancement, personal growth, and joy.

Having a token of confidence can override the sense of inadequacy that may come from negative memories, refocusing your mind on a positive memory of self-belief. When you associate a symbol with your ability to overcome self-doubt and achieve an ambitious goal, that symbol activates your confidence to take on new goals. The symbol can give you an instant psychological boost.

A token of confidence is living proof that you've overcome before, and you can overcome again.

This psychological boost comes from a shift in mindset. By reminding you that you have the psychological resources within you to overcome challenges and make progress, your token of confidence encourages you to continue pursuing your goals. It fuels your drive to push your limits, allowing the present version of yourself—not the previous version stuck in negative past memories—to define the limits of your ability.

By redefining your limits, a token of confidence encourages you to continually seek new challenges and opportunities for growth. It instills a growth mindset where your instinct is to *approach* challenges rather than avoid them. It reminds you that your potential isn't fixed; it's always able to expand.

HOW TO FIND YOUR TOKEN OF CONFIDENCE

Chances are, you already have items in your life that can serve as tokens of confidence without even realizing it. It's just a matter of recognizing what those items truly mean to you and appreciating their significance as symbols of your abilities.

Finding your token of confidence involves reflecting on the journey you took to get where you are today, identifying significant milestones along the way, and recognizing objects that symbolize your achievements and your growth in meeting those milestones. A token of confidence should hold personal significance, meaning more to you than to anyone else. It should instinctively remind you of your past and your resilience in overcoming adversity. It should symbolize your strength and represent the unique experiences that define who you are.

You can have just one token of confidence or dozens of them. There's no limit. Here's a step-by-step guide to help you discover and make the most of your first token of confidence.

Step 1: Reflect on Your Achievements

The first step is to reflect on your past achievements. Consider any moments when you faced challenges and overcame them. Think about times when you felt proud of yourself, accomplished something meaningful, or pushed yourself beyond what you thought were your limits. Think of something you've done that you—or someone else—thought you'd never be able to do. Ask yourself, "What moments in my life have defined who I am, built my resilience, and made me feel most capable?"

Your achievements can be in any area of life. They might include:

- **Academic Achievements.** Earning a degree, passing a challenging class, getting a scholarship, or receiving an award
- **Professional Achievements.** Getting a promotion, getting a dream job, completing a challenging project, launching a business, or learning a new skill
- **Personal Achievements.** Overcoming a fear or phobia, quitting smoking, or learning a new language
- **Creative Achievements.** Completing a piece of artwork, publishing your writing, or participating in a theater or dance performance
- **Athletic Achievements.** Running a marathon, winning a sports competition, or setting a new personal record
- **Life Stage Achievements.** Becoming a parent, moving to a new city, overcoming the grief of losing a loved one, or recovering from a serious illness

Step 2: Recognize Meaningful Objects

Next, think about physical objects associated with these achievements and milestones. These objects should remind you of your journey toward that achievement. They can be generic objects anyone would recognize (like a finisher's medal from a marathon) or highly personal objects only you would appreciate (like the stopwatch you used to time your practice runs). It could be a diploma, a tool or handbook that helped you master a skill, a piece of artwork you created, an item of clothing you wore during a significant experience, or *anything* that speaks to you and ties you to the memory of the achievement. Choose one of these objects to be your first token of confidence.

For instance, my main token of confidence is my guitar. It symbolizes my ability to overcome others' expectations and define for myself what I'm capable of. Another token of confidence I have is my first U.S. Open gold medal in table tennis. This medal, always on the top shelf of my bookcase, represents my ability to achieve long-term goals and perform at a high level during intense pressure.

It really doesn't matter which specific object you choose as your token of confidence. What matters is that it symbolizes the journey, effort, and perseverance that led to your achievement.

Step 3: Ensure Positive Personal Significance

When choosing your token of confidence, make sure it holds personal significance and resonates with you on a deep level. It should bring up feelings of pride, resilience, and accomplishment whenever you see it. The personal connection you have with the object is what gives it its power as a token of confidence.

Ask yourself these three questions:

1. Does this object remind me of my journey toward something meaningful in my life?
2. Does it make me feel positive?
3. Does it remind me of my ability to stay resilient, overcome challenges, and grow?

If you answer yes to each of these questions, then you've found a token of confidence.

HARNESSING YOUR TOKEN OF CONFIDENCE

Once you've identified your token of confidence, place it somewhere you'll see it often as you go about your day. It could be displayed on your desk, on a shelf or wall in your living room, in your car, or any other place you frequently spend time. Keeping your token visible serves as a consistent reminder of your capabilities. In moments of self-doubt, it's just a glance away that can redirect your thoughts from doubt toward belief.

Whenever you doubt yourself, let your token of confidence be just a glance away—ready to shift your thoughts from self-doubt to self-belief.

Use your token of confidence to craft a story arc of growth and resilience in your life. Author your own story and remember: Your token isn't about the outcome; it's about the process. It's about believing in yourself and your ability to pursue anything that interests you without holding yourself back.

By reflecting on a previous milestone in your life, you remind yourself that you're capable of overcoming adversity and emerging stronger from it. This narrative can be incredibly empowering as it provides a sense of capability and progress. When self-doubt begins to creep in, revisiting this narrative by viewing your token can disrupt negative dialogue with evidence of your competence and resilience. It makes you feel empowered.

Your token of confidence can also serve as a foundation for setting new goals. Reflect on how far you've come and trust in your ability to determine where you'd like to go next. Recall the feelings of struggle and doubt you've felt in the past and the journey you took to overcome those barriers and achieve your goal. This reflection can help lessen the weight of self-doubt in the present moment and motivate you to tackle new challenges with confidence.

Over time, find new tokens of confidence in your life. Build up a collection of them. Each new milestone and moment of resilience can add to your collection of tokens, portraying your life as an ongoing journey of growth and self-improvement.

Ultimately, tokens of confidence anchor you in your past successes, providing a solid foundation on which to build present and future confidence. They're constant reminders that you're capable, resilient, and worthy of success. By keeping your tokens visible and appreciating them on a regular basis, you can counteract self-doubt and cultivate an inquisitive mindset of continuous self-discovery and empowerment.

CONFIDENCE, DISTILLED

Tokens of Confidence Are Symbols of Ability. Tokens of confidence are symbols representing your achievements, overcoming obstacles, and personal growth. They serve as reminders of your capabilities and limitless potential.

Tokens Provide Inspiration Through Doubt. Having a token of confidence provides a tangible source of inspiration and motivation, especially during times of doubt or difficulty.

Keep Your Tokens Visible for Regular Reflection. Regularly reflecting on your tokens of confidence helps shift your mindset from self-doubt to self-belief, giving you a powerful confidence boost.

FINAL THOUGHTS: STEPPING INTO CONFIDENCE

Confidence isn't something you can find out in the world or stumble upon by chance; it's a power that lies within you. It's a mindset you can develop, nurture, and strengthen over time. It's a mentality you can unleash and a version of yourself you can step into.

As you become more confident, you express yourself and pursue your goals with less self-doubt. You show the world who you really are without holding yourself back. You view your dreams and ambitions as worthwhile pursuits that are within reach, believing in yourself while you chase after your goals. You apply the full meaning of the confidence equation:

Strategic Vulnerability
+ Adaptive Resilience
+ Inquisitive Self-Discovery

CONFIDENCE

These are the three keys to unleashing your inner confidence as an introvert: strategic vulnerability, adaptive resilience, and inquisitive self-discovery. Understanding these keys lets you solve your own confidence equation, cracking your mind's code for confidence. Each chapter in this book has provided you with the insights, tools, and strategies you need to handle these keys with clarity and purpose. Now, let's bring it all together:

KEY 1: STRATEGIC VULNERABILITY

Vulnerability is often misunderstood as a weakness, but it's truly a source of great strength. Embracing vulnerability strategically allows you to connect with yourself and others on a deeper level, fostering a more authentic form of confidence.

Your differences are assets. Your uniqueness is what makes you special, and recognizing and celebrating your differences are crucial for building confidence. When you embrace your unique strengths instead of conforming to the status quo, you can define yourself on your own terms. You can transform perceived weaknesses into surprising advantages. Leverage your individuality to create a distinct path that sets you apart and empowers you to thrive.

By owning your struggle, you can own your story. Acknowledging when you've suffered, felt hurt, or been wronged is an essential part of healing and moving forward. It's important to allow yourself to feel and process your emotions without judgment. Accepting your struggles as legitimate and acknowledging the impact they've had on you allow you to develop self-compassion and inner growth. Embracing the ways in which you feel like a victim while becoming the hero of your own story fosters an empowering mindset that combines the healing power of vulnerability with the strength of resilience.

By stepping into vulnerability, you create space for genuine self-love. You allow yourself to be open and honest about your feelings, experiences, and struggles. You allow yourself to be seen for who you truly are, fostering a sense of self-acceptance and self-worth. Instead of hiding your insecurities, use them as a way to live authentically and connect more meaningfully with others.

The ability to improvise is a powerful tool. Life is unpredictable, and being able to adapt and think on your feet can stop self-doubt from creeping in. Improvisation teaches you to trust your instincts, take risks, and embrace the unknown with a positive attitude. It encourages creativity and spontaneity, allowing you to navigate life's challenges with ease. It reveals that true confidence comes from accepting and adapting to the present moment, not from rigid preparation. Let go of fixed agendas, respond to new situations with curiosity, and cultivate a "yes, and" mindset.

KEY 2: ADAPTIVE RESILIENCE

Your resilience lets you bounce back from adversity and keep moving forward despite challenges. It allows you to maintain your belief in yourself in the face of setbacks, choosing to persevere rather than stagnate.

Resilience in the face of doubt is essential. Doubt—whether it comes from within yourself or from others—can be a significant obstacle to confidence. Learning to trust yourself and your abilities, even when others don't, is vital. Embrace doubt as a natural part of any journey and recognize that other people's doubts usually say more about their own insecurities than they say about your potential. Recognize these projections and focus on your own capabilities. Don't take doubt personally; use it as motivation to prove to yourself what you're capable of.

Staying cool under pressure is another core component of resilience that underlies confidence. Life will throw unexpected challenges your way, and staying calm and composed can make all the difference. Practice techniques like mindfulness, meditation, and deep breathing to help manage anxiety and prevent your mind from spiraling. Regular mindfulness meditation helps quiet your ego, detaching you from dwelling on the past and worrying about the future. When you're able to stay mentally present, you can quiet self-doubt and keep your confidence intact even in the highest pressure of situations. By mastering your response to pressure, you can maintain a steady and versatile sense of confidence anywhere you go.

Growing from rejection is a third element of resilience. Rejection is an inevitable part of life, and how you respond to it can shape your confidence—for better or for worse. Instead of seeing rejection as a failure, view it as a learning opportunity that signals a natural step on the path toward your goal. Remember that you're not defined by the outcomes of your pursuits but by the efforts you put into them. Rejection doesn't erase your worth; it reveals your resilience. Every rejection is both a mirror for growth and a gift you've yet to unwrap.

Rethinking tragedy is a powerful mental shift for building resilience. Tragedy and setbacks can weigh you down, but they also create space for introspection and profound growth. By rethinking how you view and respond to hardship, you can find strength and resilience in life's most challenging moments. In the process, even painful emotions become sources of energy, guiding you toward reflection, healing, and renewed motivation. Hidden within the pain of tragedy may be a new pillar of confidence, waiting to give you the strength you need to move forward.

KEY 3: INQUISITIVE SELF-DISCOVERY

Self-discovery is the art of understanding and embracing all aspects of yourself, including your strengths, weaknesses, values, passions, and imagination. This journey of self-awareness, self-acceptance, and ruthless authenticity is crucial for building genuine confidence.

Reconnecting with your inner child is a critical step toward inquisitive self-discovery. Reconnecting with your inner child means embracing the curiosity, spontaneity, and playfulness that you had as a young child. Allow yourself to be silly, expressive, and explore things on a whim for no clear reason at all. Engage in activities that bring you joy and make you feel creative, unbound by restrictions. Carve out opportunities for play all around your life. Recognize that adulthood is a performance that suppresses your inner child. It's in your hands to perform less and live more. Your inner child is an unbounded source of confidence as it's a part of you free from self-doubt. It's always within you, lending you a mindset you can channel at any time. Start channeling it more often.

By quieting your social comparisons, you gain a clearer view of yourself and an inquisitive appreciation for your individuality. It's easy to fall into the trap of comparing yourself to others. However, these unfairly biased comparisons often lead to feelings of inadequacy and self-doubt. Choose self-comparison over social comparison; focus on your own journey and celebrate your unique achievements, measuring your progress against your past self. Recognize that everyone's path is different, and your worth isn't determined by how you measure up to others.

Embracing humor is another important element of inquisitive self-discovery. Humor helps you navigate difficult situations, accept who you are, and maintain a positive outlook during times of adversity. Reject the myth of maturity and find a sense of humor within your inner child by allowing yourself to be playful, spontaneous, and imperfect. Laugh at your mistakes, share funny stories with others, and enjoy the lighter side of life. Humor isn't a skill; it's a mindset. When you choose not to take yourself too seriously, your sense of humor can be a constant source of strength and confidence.

Keep a token of confidence. Lastly, to remind yourself of your capabilities, keep a token of confidence: a physical object that symbolize your achievements, personal growth, and overcoming obstacles. These tokens serve as tangible reminders of the progress you've made in life. They're symbols indicating that you're capable of pursuing any goal you put your mind to. Identify your own tokens of confidence and keep them in a place where you can see them regularly. Whether it's a memento from an accomplishment, a note of encouragement, or a small object that holds personal significance, these tokens can inspire you and remind you of your inner strength. They counteract self-doubt and allow you to redefine your own abilities.

A MORE CONFIDENT YOU

As you step into confidence, remember that it's a continuous journey. You'll have moments of self-doubt, and that's perfectly normal. But with the tools and insights you've gained through reading this book, you're well-equipped to face them. Self-doubt itself isn't something to fear; it's how you respond to that doubt that matters. The more effectively you apply the keys of the confidence equation, the more you'll train your mind to quiet down self-doubts automatically when they do occur, giving them less and less power over you.

Continue to lean into vulnerability, trust your resilience, and cultivate self-discovery. Each day of your life, you're constantly evolving into who you are. There's always more of yourself to discover and new opportunities and challenges to weather while accepting and celebrating the highs and lows of your experience.

I didn't find my own confidence from surviving the ICU or earning a PhD. I didn't win it in any table tennis tournament or comedy contest. I unleashed it bit by bit through everything in between—by staying true to myself, growing from every challenge, and discovering the person I've always wanted to be.

ACKNOWLEDGMENTS

This book would not exist without the support of two extraordinary people. To my brilliant literary agent, Laura Yorke, thank you for championing my story from the very beginning and for your unwavering belief in me. I'm grateful each day to have you in my corner. To my exceptional editor, Christine Belleris, thank you for amplifying my voice and helping bring this book to life. Working with you has been an absolute pleasure.

ABOUT THE AUTHOR

DAN ROSENFELD, PhD, is an award-winning psychologist, table tennis player, and comedian.

Dr. Rosenfeld holds a PhD in psychology from UCLA, where he is currently a post-doctoral scholar. He has published over forty peer-reviewed articles in leading scientific journals, and his work has been featured in *The Wall Street Journal, The Atlantic,* and on NPR. Dr. Rosenfeld has received multiple national research awards from the American Psychological Association, including the prestigious Junior Scientist Fellowship.

Dr. Rosenfeld is also a two-time U.S. Open Table Tennis gold medalist and a former member of the U.S. National Table Tennis Team. He has performed stand-up comedy at popular venues around Los Angeles and won first place in the U.S. Comedy Contest. Additionally, Dr. Rosenfeld is founder and director of The Match Lab, where he has coached over 500 clients on how to improve their dating lives.

Born with cerebral palsy, Dr. Rosenfeld spent his childhood in intensive physical rehabilitation. He spent hundreds of hours in physical therapy learning how to walk, in speech therapy learning how to talk, and in occupational therapy learning how to live independently. Proudly an introvert himself, Dr. Rosenfeld is passionate about empowering introverts to overcome self-doubt, harness their unique strengths, and embrace their authentic selves.